A HIKER'S HISTORY *of the* APPALACHIAN TRAIL

A HIKER'S HISTORY *of the* APPALACHIAN TRAIL

MILLS KELLY

Published by The History Press
An imprint of Arcadia Publishing
Charleston, SC
www.historypress.com

Cover image: Hikers on Mary's Rock (Virginia), 1930. *Potomac Appalachian Trail Club Archives, used with permission.*

First published 2025

Manufactured in the United States

ISBN 9781467159999
Hardcover ISBN 9781540299840

Library of Congress Control Number: 2025941120

For my three favorite hiking partners:
Susan, Ross and Spencer.

CONTENTS

ACKNOWLEDGEMENTS

This book began in 2016, when I first had the idea of writing a history of the Appalachian Trail from the perspective of hikers instead of focusing on the trail's founders, builders and maintainers. It just seemed to me that the histories of the trail that already existed all but ignored the people who actually hike on the trail, and I decided to reclaim their voices and their experiences as essential to the trail's history. Between then and now, so many archivists, trail club leaders and hikers have done their best to help me navigate the historical record, make sense of what I found and begin to tell the story that it would be impossible to name them all. Some of the most helpful along the way have been Becky Fullerton, archivist of the Appalachian Mountain Club; Ken Wise (now retired), who helped me navigate the archives of the Smoky Mountains Hiking Club; Diana Christopoulos, archivist and past president of the Roanoke Appalachian Trail Club; and, most of all, Brian King (also retired), longtime archivist and publicist of the Appalachian Trail Conservancy. Without their help—and the help of so many others—this book would not exist.

I also want to say a special thanks to Sandy Moyer, Jerry Johnson and Becky Foreman, devoted volunteers at the Appalachian Trail Museum in Pine Grove Furnace, Pennsylvania, who have been digitizing trail shelter registers for years now. Digital copies of those shelter registers have been essential sources for this book, and without them, it would have been so much harder to tell this story. Larry Luxembourg, Julie Queen and Kurt Bodling at the museum generously made all the museum's collections fully available to me as I did my best to understand the hiker experience over the past one hundred years. Several trail friends have provided encouragement, critiques and inspiration along the way—Jeff Ryan, Sarah (Dips) Robison and, most of all, Sarah Jones Decker, who embraced my project, and me, offering up free stays at her family's beautiful farm in Marshall, North Carolina, over many years and incorporating me into her family along the way. Sarah is an amazing photographer, and several of her images are in the color insert.

I received a faculty development grant from George Mason University at an early stage of the project, and my friend Professor Andreas Fickers, director of the Centre for Contemporary and Digital History at the University of Luxembourg, gave me space and time to get the writing process started in earnest in 2024. The German-American Fulbright Commission made it possible for me to spend five wonderful months in Mainz, Germany, teaching at Johannes Gutenberg University. When I wasn't teaching, I was writing the initial draft of this book.

For three years, I worked with an incredible team of people on *The Green Tunnel* podcast, which ultimately totaled fifty-one episodes. My thinking about the trail's history crystallized during our work together and through more than one hundred interviews for that show. To all these friends, supporters and sponsors, I can't thank you enough. This book wouldn't exist without you.

In the mountains
The mind becomes
A heart

—Richard Harrison, 2023

INTRODUCTION

It's the 6th day of a 10-day hike. My experienced hiker boyfriend talked me into my first camping-hiking trip. Definitely a vacation to remember! We've hiked approximately 52 miles so far. My feet don't understand what's happening to them! It rained our first three days—great first impression of the forest—but it's been sunny the past three. All the shelters have been clean and comfortable. I love the scenic overlooks—my camera has been working overtime! I heard many horror stories about bears, but so far they've run away from us...could it be our "perfume"? Well, it's dinner time. Gotta go!

—*shelter register, Virginia, 1983**

Sometime in the summer of 1971, I set foot on the Appalachian Trail (AT) for the first time. I was an almost twelve-year-old Boy Scout on my very first backpacking trip. Because I lived in the Northern Virginia suburbs of Washington, D.C., Shenandoah National Park was less than two hours away by car, so that's where my troop went backpacking. Our Scoutmaster at the time was a middle-aged man named Mr. Ballard, a retired marine who had fought his way across the Pacific during the Second World War and who believed that the only way boys truly got something out of Scouting was to go backpacking. If Mr. Ballard knew that the AT

* Throughout the book, I cite entries or portions of entries from various trail shelter registers. I identify them by state and year rather than specific location to preserve some limited anonymity for the authors of those entries.

stretched from Georgia to Maine, he failed to mention it. For my entire first year as a hiker and a backpacker, I thought the "Appalachian Trail" was just the name of the trail we hiked on in the park.

In many ways, my 1970s version of the AT was not much different from the one you can hike today in Shenandoah National Park. It was a relatively wide, well-trodden trail rolling over ridges and crisscrossing back and forth across Skyline Drive. There were old stone and beam shelters where we spent the night when we could, cramming as many of us as possible into the bunks and sitting around the fire pits at night. Sometimes scruffy long-distance hikers would share the shelters with us. Those were still the days of hippie culture, so seeing someone in cutoff jeans with long hair and a beard, or a woman with long braids and a tie-dye T-shirt, was an everyday sight in my world. But those hikers did seem to know a lot more about backpacking than we did, and they were always happy when we offered to share some of our food.

My first backpack was a horror. My parents had taken me to the local navy surplus store to gear up, and the pack I bought there had a steel frame, a canvas body and hard leather straps and weighed a ton. I also bought a pup tent that was little more than a rain fly (no doors, leaky floor), a heavy cloth and fiberfill sleeping bag and a Vietnam War surplus mess kit made from tin. My first boots were also military surplus and well used by someone before me. Just that base gear must have weighed almost as much as the entire set of gear plus food I take with me on the trail today, and it was all my twelve-year-old body could lug up and down those mountains. But I loved everything about it. It was *mine*, and it gave me access to the wilderness in ways that nothing else could.

My whole view of the Appalachian Trail changed the following year. A recently retired government official named Ed Garvey lived just around the corner from where our Boy Scout troop met, and in the fall of 1972, he came to one of our meetings to give a talk about his new book, *Appalachian Hiker: Adventure of a Lifetime*. That book, the first book-length account of a thru hike of the AT, is credited by many with supercharging the boom in thru hiking that has long since washed over the Appalachian Trail, but at that moment, it was a revelation to me. As Garvey showed us slides from his hike, it dawned on me that the trail I'd been backpacking on for a year or so went *all the way to Georgia and all the way to Maine*. I couldn't believe it. A trail of more than two thousand miles. A path that could take me to Atlanta, where my mother's family lived, or to Maine, which was just a dim concept to me in those days. Something awoke inside me that evening, and the next time we went to the trail, I remember standing at one of the concrete mileposts so typical of Shenandoah National Park and looking first south and then north, imagining what it would be like to hike those two thousand miles by myself.

That desire stuck with me. These days, tens of thousands of people have the same dreamy notion of thru hiking the AT, and each spring, two to three thousand give it a go. But in 1972, thru hiking was still a fringe idea. Fewer than 150 hikers completed a thru hike that year and only a few more the following year. It just wasn't something many people did and even fewer talked about. But I kept dreaming about it. I saved my money. I went to our local backpacking store—Appalachian Outfitters in Oakton, Virginia—and fondled all the gear, eventually getting rid of my original kit and replacing it with a then modern external frame JanSport pack that weighed about one-third of what my navy-surplus pack weighed, a down sleeping bag, a SVEA 123 white gas stove and a much better tent. As soon as I could drive, I would head for the trail either alone or with a friend for weekend trips. During my senior year of high school, I hiked something like half of the trail in Shenandoah, and in my college application essays, I declared that when I graduated from college I planned to "do something really impossible. I will hike the entire Appalachian Trail in one year."

Except that I didn't. Like for so many AT hikers, my dream of completing the trail remained a dream. I got busy with jobs, new friends, getting married and moving overseas and then around the country for work. We had children—children who set foot on the Appalachian Trail for the first time at ages four and two—who consumed most of my free time. People ask me all the time, "Have you hiked the whole thing?" My reply is, "No, I've only hiked a little over 600 miles of the trail." Unless they're serious long-distance hikers, "a little over 600 miles" sounds like a lot of hiking. But that's only slightly more than 25 percent of the AT. Over the years, I've come to realize that thru hikes are not the thing the Appalachian Trail exists for. A thru hike is a monumental achievement, worthy of praise, but it is just one of the hundreds if not thousands of ways hikers spend time on America's most iconic long-distance hiking trail. Thru hikes just happen to be what people seem to want to talk about the most.

The Appalachian Trail turns one hundred in 2025. For some reason, we assign special significance to centennials in our society, so 2025 seems to be the right moment to look back at the history of *all* the many ways hikers have spent time on the trail that Benton MacKaye first proposed in 1921. There are several good histories of the AT, but those books all tell the story from one perspective: the perspective of those who conceived of, built

Potomac Appalachian Trail Club hikers at Centerpoint Knob, Pennsylvania, 1940. *Appalachian Trail Conservancy Archives*.

and maintained the trail. And those are important stories. The history of the Appalachian Trail as a recreational resource is a remarkable tale of vision, perseverance, the transformation of the trail from an all-volunteer project to a national park and the more present struggles to preserve the trail's ecosystem in the face of encroaching development, climate change, substantial cuts in government funding and, in some sections, significant overuse. Without the vision and the sweat of so many women and men, almost all of them volunteers, the Appalachian Trail wouldn't exist. Understanding the story of their vision and their long labor on behalf of the trail and its hikers is very important. But as important as those individuals and themes are, they leave out the *most* important characters in the story: the hikers for whom the trail was created in the first place. For those who want more details about the building and maintenance of the trail, I have included some suggested reading at the end of the book.

This book tells the history of the Appalachian Trail from the bottom up—from the perspective of hikers rather than from the perspective of the trail builders. According to the National Park Service, somewhere between 3 million and 4 million people set foot on the Appalachian Trail every year, most for a few hours and a significant fraction for a day, a few days or even a few weeks. Less than 0.5 percent of all those hikers are attempting a thru hike. But these days, what we know about hiking on the Appalachian Trail over the past one hundred years comes to us mostly from thru hikers. The reason for this imbalance is fairly straightforward. Some fraction of those who manage to hike more than two thousand miles in one hiking season feel compelled to tell *their* story. Ed Garvey was the first, but now there are dozens and dozens of books about thru hikes of the AT, and in this age of social media, there is a virtual thru hiking media ecosystem of its own—YouTube channels, Instagram feeds, podcasts, Facebook groups and pages and countless magazine articles, blogs and other rivers of text telling the story of "my hike." The hero journey is a trope in western literature, and most of those thru hike stories fit the trope very nicely. Ever since the ancient Greeks, we've loved reading about the optimism, the struggles, the emotional crises and eventually the successful resolution of the hero's tale. Whether it's Odysseus's epic journey home from the siege of Troy or speed hiker Jennifer Pharr Davis's *Becoming Odyssa: Adventures on the Appalachian Trail*, the basic story is largely the same. The hero overcomes obstacle after obstacle, eventually reaching his or her final destination, and is transformed in some way by the experience. We love stories of hero journeys because they allow us to live the journey vicariously without, for instance, having our eyelids

Hiking the Appalachian Trail in Maine, 1939. *Appalachian Trail Conservancy Archives.*

freeze in an ice storm, as happened to Davis on her first thru hike, or because we believe there are important lessons in those stories that we can apply to our own lives.

Hikers who go to the Appalachian Trail for a few hours or a few days don't write books about those experiences, and frankly, if they did, who would read them? What's so epic about the three hours my wife and I spent hiking a five-mile loop to a beautiful overlook and then back to the car? As a result, when historians write about Appalachian Trail hikers, they almost always default to sources produced by thru hikers, with the result that we learn the story of the Appalachian Trail hiker from the perspective of those who represent a tiny, tiny fraction of the millions of hikers who set foot on the AT each year. The experiences and stories of thru hikers are very important to the history of the hiker experience on the Appalachian Trail, and they are not ignored in this book. But thru hikers are only one very small part of a very big story, a story that deserves to be told just as much as the epic journey of an individual thru hiker or the section hiker who finally knits together the last of their sections and completes the entire trail.

What makes telling the big story difficult, of course, is that day hikers and shorter-distance hikers didn't write books about their experiences and, these days, don't have large social media feeds devoted to that hike they took last weekend. Fortunately, the archives of the Appalachian Trail are filled with sources about the hiking experiences of the 99.5 percent of AT hikers who didn't attempt or complete a thru hike. There are many different archival collections devoted to the trail, including those of the Appalachian Trail Conservancy (ATC), the more than thirty trail-maintaining clubs, the various federal and state agencies with a stake in the AT and the collection at the Appalachian Trail Museum in Pennsylvania. Of the many sources in those archives, the most useful for understanding the experiences of average hikers are the ATC collection, some of the trail club archives and the AT Museum library and archives. These organizations hold copies of newsletters that focus on local hikers rather than thru hikers, letters from hikers detailing their experiences on the trail over the decades and many, many photographs from those hikes.

But when it comes to really getting inside the experience of non-thru hikers, the most important source of all is the registers the trail clubs left in trailside shelters and cabins for hikers to write in. Unfortunately, those registers, dating back to the 1930s, have been kept only haphazardly. Some trail clubs don't keep them at all, others keep a few and some of the clubs have done their best to keep them all. Many hundreds of the registers exist, scattered across the archives and the decades, and none is available online. If you want to know what it was like to hike on the Appalachian Trail in 1937, 1952, 1969 or 1983, you have to go to those archives and read the newsletters and the letters, look at the photographs and read the trail shelter registers the old-fashioned way.

I've spent much of the past several years reading club newsletters, letters hikers sent the clubs or the ATC about their hikes and, most importantly, those shelter registers to try to get a clearer picture of what it was like to hike on the Appalachian Trail over the decades. Those sources offer many more insights into the experiences of all hikers than one can ever get from reading just a few thru hiker accounts or by watching some YouTube videos. After all, the fundamental idea for the Appalachian Trail was that it was to be a place where the toilers in the great cities of America's Eastern Seaboard could get away for a few hours or perhaps a few days to get some fresh air, breathe in the scents of the mountains, hear birds singing and perhaps see some of the many wild animals that populate the Appalachian Mountains. Through these experiences, those hikers might

21

10/27 Friday Day hike ē Mike. Sunny and warm. The way North has some Nice views. Like to spend more time here but the trail calls — Oggy

10·28 Only 16 A.T. miles to go! (14 today, 2 on Sunday). Nice night on the deck beside the fire pit. Probably the last night under the stars this year. No more noisy insects or moving [illegible] or leaves falling on my face. 7 months & 1 week on the A.T. & some of it has been fun, all of it a great experience. Hope you all gain something from your experience of the A.T. May your god go with you.

Mad Dog '83

P.S. I also had the best hiking buddy – Hokey Pokey – that a cranky old dog could ever ask for. Thanks, H.P.

10/28 What is normal? A different place to sleep each nite or my bed at home. Eating everything and anything or a controlled diet. A day consisting of eating, sleeping, hiking or a day full of a myriad of activities and people. I am ready for the journey to end but will miss this routine and simple life. Seven months a long time a good time. Lessons learned? Thats something I'll work out later

Hokey Pokey 2000'

P.S. Mans best friend, Mad Dog. An intelligent and amusing breed.

10/28 Couldn't find anything to carry water in. Peed on fire. Might not want to cook on that for a few days. Enjoy!

Page from a trail shelter register, 1983. *Appalachian Trail Museum Archives.*

find some peace in a chaotic world, might improve their health and might find a kind of joy in reconnecting with the natural world. In other words, the Appalachian Trail was not intended to be a place for epic journeys. It was intended to be a place where individuals might find solace, healing and ways to solve what AT founder Benton MacKaye called "the problem of living" in a modern industrial society. Since its completion in the late 1930s, the AT has been all of those things to countless millions of people. That the Appalachian Trail also became a place where a small number of hikers embarked on epic journeys isn't a bad thing at all. It's just that those journeys are one piece of a much larger and more complex story. To help make it clear who I am talking about in the pages that follow, unless I use the terms *thru hiker* or *long-distance hiker*, I am discussing the 99.5 percent of AT hikers who weren't on an epic journey.

One thing that has become clear to me, to the degree that anything in the historical record can be clear, is that Appalachian Trail hikers who aren't on an epic journey have gone and still go to the trail for the very reasons Benton MacKaye first hoped they would. They want exercise. They want

On the way to Mizpah Hut, New Hampshire, 1979. *Appalachian Mountain Club Archives.*

fresh air. They want to engage in what the Japanese call "forest bathing." They wanted and still want to get away from the noise, the pollution, the stress, the phone calls and eventually the e-mails, the text messages, the traffic and, most importantly, the frenetic pace of life in America and, increasingly, around the world. For most hikers, walking on a mountain trail forces you to slow down, whether you want to or not. Only the most athletic can keep up a brisk pace on a steeply sloping mountain path, and in my experience, even the most athletic hikers tend to slow down after a while for the simple reason that they want to look around to see that bird calling from a tree up above, to pause to look at the pinkish-purple wild gardenias blooming in casual profusion where the sun breaks through to the forest floor, to sit for just a minute on a rock beside a rushing stream and just stare at the water as it gurgles past or to stop and watch as a mother deer and her two fauns stroll across the trail up ahead. These are the experiences hikers have been going in search of on the Appalachian Trail for the past one hundred years, and their joy in being in wild places bubbles up from their letters and their register entries:

> *"We walked for an hour under some of the largest and most beautiful oak trees I've ever seen."*

> *"It rained on us for the entire day, but we still had fun. The forest is so beautiful."*
>
> *"The shelter has SKINKS! Even ones with red heads!"*
>
> *"I saw a bobcat!!!"*

Their joy in nature, in the brief moments where they reach out and touch the wild and are transformed, would have brought MacKaye and the other founders of the trail much happiness. It was to make those experiences possible that they created a trail of more than two thousand miles in the first place. These emotional moments haven't changed much in one hundred years, and I hope that as you read on, you'll find some of yourself in the words of the many AT hikers quoted in the pages that follow. Whether you've hiked on the Appalachian Trail for a few hours, a few days or for months, this is your history.

A SHORT HISTORY OF HIKING

Afoot and light-hearted I take to the open road,
Healthy, free, the world before me,
The long brown path before me leading wherever I choose.
—Walt Whitman, "Song of the Open Road," 1856

Americans are, or were, a walking people. When European settlers came to North America and began pushing the continent's original residents aside, they found the paths that Indigenous people had made over the many millennia of their residence in North America and thought them useful. Like their Indigenous predecessors, those settlers walked by necessity unless they were prosperous enough to own a horse or a mule. As they walked on paths laid down by Indigenous people, they widened and leveled some of those trails enough that they could accommodate horse- or mule-drawn wagons and eventually carriages. A substantial fraction of the road network of North America sits atop those old and sometimes ancient paths, and an even larger fraction of the hiking trails we enjoy today likewise sit atop those paths.

Until the late nineteenth century, Americans did very little walking for pleasure on the trails and roads they created. Instead, they walked to get from one place to another, to get goods to market, to hunt and fish or to reach places where food and medicinal plants were predictably found. They visited neighbors and went to church. They fled north, emancipating themselves from enslavement. They marched in armies or followed armies in the field.

But the late nineteenth century was a time of great change in Americans' walking habits. As the country industrialized, more and more people moved into the increasingly densely packed cities where the mills, the factories and the jobs were. Omnibuses began transporting people across those cities. Railroads soon began transporting ever greater numbers of people between cities. Trolleys, first drawn by horses but eventually powered by electricity, made it easier and easier for urban dwellers to avoid walking. By the end of the century, Americans were walking less and less for the simple reason that they didn't need to. And, of course, in the twentieth century, the automobile made walking even less necessary. But those settlers didn't just walk to get from one place to another. Some of them also found joy in walking. Henry David Thoreau, one of America's most famous walkers, exhorted his readers, "We should go forth on the shortest walk, perchance, in the spirit of undying adventure, never to return."

The increasing concentration of the American population in cities ironically led to a growth in walking for pleasure. Sometime after the Civil War, middle-class residents of America's cities began to engage in organized walking. What began as a form of promenading slowly morphed into something more focused on the health and sometimes religious benefits of time spent exercising in the outdoors. As more people began taking part in organized walking, city dwellers began to shape their urban spaces to provide access to greenspaces, places where walking felt more like it involved time in nature even if it was still in a city. The most famous of the urban greenspaces developed in the nineteenth century was New York's Central Park. Begun in 1858, the huge park in the center of the city, which required displacing poor Black residents to construct, took fifteen years to complete and was a hit with the public almost immediately. Like its predecessor, Boston's Public Garden, Central Park became a place not only for the wealthy and the prosperous to promenade but also for members of the middle class to walk for pleasure. Inspired by the success of these two great urban parks, planners in places like Philadelphia, Chicago, Atlanta, Baltimore, Washington, D.C., and many other American cities began to lay out parks, some of which, like Rock Creek Park in Washington, retained at least some of their natural wildness.

According to historian Silas Chamberlin, these urban parks "provided the ideal places to walk because they offered predictable and well-scripted nature experiences near urban residents." The parks were green, filled with trees and sometimes streams, rock formations and other tame avatars of the wilder side of North America. They were easy to get to and offered at least the illusion that one had left the confines of the city—with its noise, its crush of people and its often foul and fetid air—for a dose of the natural world. The growing availability of these pleasant walking opportunities helped spawn walking clubs, which provided members with structured and well-planned opportunities to walk together for exercise and health but also to learn about the natural world. Quite often a hike in an urban park or large cemetery might be led by a teacher, a professor or a scientist who could educate participants on local flora and fauna, the geology of the region or the ways that weather altered the natural environment. These clubs were almost entirely the domain of the educated, the prosperous and the White residents of America's cities, people who had the leisure time necessary to take part in activities like walking for pleasure. Women, however, were *not* excluded from these clubs. Right from the start of the organized hiking movement, the clubs that sprang up across the country encouraged the participation of women, and in many cases, female membership far outnumbered male membership.

Soon, though, urban walking in carefully scripted natural spaces just didn't seem like quite enough. According to Chamberlin, toward the end of the nineteenth century, an odd thing began to happen. Just at the moment when middle-class Americans had achieved a measure of safety and comfort in their lives, they started coming up with ways to experience physical hardships that their newfound prosperity had largely eliminated. Instead of continuing to hike in those well-ordered and carefully designed urban parks, members of the hiking public began going to actual forests and mountains to hike for pleasure, climbing mountains, often at great risk, and exploring the waste places of the far north for scientific purposes and personal glory; they camped out in nature in rough tents or lean-to cabins purpose-built for a back-to-nature experience. Going off into nature in these ways gave at least some middle-class American men opportunities to reaffirm their masculinity at a time when it seemed to be slipping away amid the creature comforts of their ever-more prosperous existence. They became, as eventual president Theodore Roosevelt famously urged, devoted to the "strenuous life" both for physical improvement and as an act of patriotism. America, they thought, needed strong and willful men, accustomed to overcoming hardship (at least on the weekends or during their vacations), so that it could take its rightful place among the great imperial powers of Europe.

When they looked for inspiration or guidance on how they should be walking in the wild, these newly adventurous hikers often looked to Thoreau, whose complete works were published posthumously between 1893 and 1906. The growing popularity of Thoreau's writing fueled a

Hikers on Blackrock Summit, Virginia, circa 1900. *National Park Service*.

revival of interest in his, and other American Transcendentalists', ideas about the natural world and man's place in it. Those who revered Thoreau not only saw hiking as an opportunity for exercise away from the cities but also believed that important messages for humanity could be found by being in the wild and reflecting on what one experienced there. It was in the forests and the mountains that men and women could learn from nature how to live better lives. By mindfully observing nature, they could find peace and renewal.

It is unlikely that many of the Thoreau enthusiasts read his essay on climbing to the summit of Mount Katahdin, now the northern terminus of the Appalachian Trail. Had they done so, they would have learned that Thoreau was much keener on quiet rambles through the relatively safe forests to be found near Boston and that when confronted with the raw power of nature on the summit of Maine's highest peak, his spirit faltered:

> *The tops of mountains are among the unfinished parts of the globe, whither it is a slight insult to the gods to climb and pry into their secrets, and try their effect on our humanity. Only daring and insolent men, perchance, go there. Simple races, as savages, do not climb mountains. Their tops are sacred and mysterious tracts never visited by them. Pomola is always angry with those who climb to the summit of Ktaadn…*
>
> *Perhaps I most fully realized that this was primeval, untamed, and forever untamable Nature, or whatever else men call it, while coming down this part of the mountain….Nature was here something savage and awful though beautiful. I looked with awe at the ground I trod on, to see what the Powers had made there, the form and fashion and material of their work…. There was clearly felt the presence of a force not bound to be kind to man. It was a place for heathenism and superstitious rites—to be inhabited by men nearer of kin to the rocks and to wild animals than we.*

This raw version of nature was probably a bit more than most hiking club members were ready for. But Thoreau's vision of the wild places of North America as liable to test the human spirit certainly must have resonated with many men and women interested in testing their own spirits in the wild. It wasn't only Transcendentalists like Thoreau and Ralph Waldo Emerson who inspired Americans to find healing and peace in the forests. Religious historian Brett Malcolm Grainger argues that when we look closely at the practices of American evangelicals in the nineteenth century, we see that they also had a considerable interest in what he called "nature

Mount Katahdin overlooking Daicey Pond, 1939. *Appalachian Trail Conservancy Archives.*

spirituality"—the idea that "the natural world was enlivened by Christ" and that by going into the forests and mountains, believers could forge stronger connections to their faith by spending time in the wild. Each of these two intellectual strands—the Transcendentalism of Thoreau and Emerson and the nature spirituality of American evangelicals—contributed in its own way to the growing popularity of hiking, backpacking, camping and other experiences in wild places.

Shifting the locus of club activities from urban parks to much wilder places in no way discouraged women from continuing to be active and vital members of these hiking clubs. Often hiking in full-length dresses and the large hats that were fashionable at the time, women continued to hike, camp and climb alongside men. The women who took part in these outdoor activities did so for many of the same reasons as men. The late nineteenth and early twentieth centuries were a time of growing interest in women's physical health, and increasingly, women were advised to exercise, often strenuously, to remain strong and healthy and to cultivate their intellects. Growing numbers of women went into the wild with men or in groups of women hiking and camping on their own. Silent films of Appalachian Trail hikers in the 1930s attest to just how involved women were in group hikes in the mountains. Not many of those films survive in the archives, but in the ones that do, women often outnumber men in the jerky, yellowing images. Photographs of group hikes on the AT tell the

Participants in the second ATC meeting visit the trail, 1928. *Appalachian Trail Conservancy Archives.*

same story. Again and again, those photographs have just as many and sometimes more women as men.

Hikers in the twentieth century didn't just hit the trail for exercise or to reconnect with nature. Many did so because they wanted to become more educated about the natural world. The interest of hikers in the scientific exploration of nature was part of a much larger flowering of interest in the natural world in America, driven by educational reformers such as Anna Botsford Comstock, Louis Agassiz, George Washington Carver and Liberty Hyde Bailey, who encouraged her students to "study nature, not books." By the 1920s, the active study of nature—that is, getting out into nature to study plants, animals, weather and ecological change rather than just reading about these things in books—was an essential part of the curriculum in most public schools in the United States. This emphasis on up close and personal study of the natural world fit nicely with the growing interest in hiking. What better way to combine the study of nature with vigorous exercise than to hit the trail?

Nature study had been a central feature of the growing popularity of hiking and backpacking since the late nineteenth century. When a group of outdoor enthusiasts in Boston came together in 1876 to form the Appalachian Mountain Club (AMC), they did so for two purposes: to help club members explore the wild places of the White Mountains in New Hampshire and to engage in the scientific exploration of nature. Their new journal, *Appalachia*, carried stories on both subjects—adventuring into the wild and scientific reports on everything from birds to geology to fish to timber. The AMC was not America's first hiking club with an emphasis on wilderness hiking, but it was one of the earliest and is now the oldest continuously operating club. Among the club's many contributions to the history of hiking was its effort to create and then maintain a more formalized network of trails in the White Mountains that hikers could use regularly, obviating the need for bushwhacking in what was often hazardous terrain. AMC members also began the practice of blazing their trails, adding directional signs at trailheads and intersections, often with mileage to the next destination or intersection, and they eventually began publishing guides to those trails. All those efforts had the effect of fixing the AMC trails in time and space—our trail is here and not there, it is this long and not that long and it can take you there but not somewhere else. Over time, the club also began building its network of huts in the Whites, a system of shelters modeled on the hut system in Switzerland. Today, the AT passes a number of those huts, and hikers on the trail love to stop over at one when they can.

The AMC on the East Coast and the Sierra Club (founded in 1892) on the West Coast became models for similar, albeit generally smaller, hiking and outing clubs. By the turn of the century, such clubs were springing up all across the United States, and these clubs shared many of the same characteristics. They had co-ed memberships; they organized hikes, backpacking, canoeing, mountaineering and camping trips; they generally had some emphasis on the scientific study of nature; and they were peopled by members of the middle class who had the time and resources to take part in their activities. Along the spine of the Appalachians, clubs such as the Philadelphia Trail Club, the Green Mountain Club, the Carolina Mountain Club and the Smoky Mountains Hiking Club were formed in cities like Philadelphia; Burlington, Vermont; Asheville, North Carolina; and Knoxville, Tennessee. These clubs mimicked the organizational structure and activities of the AMC and, in the case of the Carolina Mountain Club, were even offshoots of that venerable club. Like their larger and more famous inspiration in New England, these smaller clubs planned numerous activities for their members, many of which had little to do with hiking or camping. While outdoor activities remained their primary reason to exist, the clubs also sponsored dinners, square dances, lectures on health and hygiene, bridge nights in the winter and even trips to the movies. Some American hiking clubs had a strong religious dimension to their activities, others were connected to local YMCA and YWCA chapters and still others sponsored Boy Scout, Girl Scout and Campfire Girl groups. Through these many activities, club members built strong friendships and reinforced their class status, and some began to work on projects related to the conservation of local forests.

Throughout the first decades of the history of the Appalachian Trail, one can find example after example of hikers reporting on the natural world they encountered along the trail—birds, mammals, amphibians, weather, plants, trees and geology. Sometimes those reports were cast in scientific terms—cataloguing which bird species the group saw on a hike in Pennsylvania or observations about the work of beavers on a pond in the Maine wilderness. But just as often, the mentions of wildlife one finds in shelter registers, letters and club newsletters are simple expressions of joy at having seen wild animals in their natural environment rather than in a zoo. Trail club leaders understood this connection between nature study and hiking because the early trail guides were filled with commentary on the natural world hikers could expect to experience on the Appalachian Trail. In their brief commentaries on their experiences in letters, newsletters and shelter registers, hikers wrote again and again about the beauty of the natural world they observed on their hikes, the challenges or thrills offered by mountain weather and especially the sightings of wild animals. Many hiked specifically for fellowship with other hikers, but most of those who ventured onto the Appalachian Trail in its early days—or at least those who wrote about their experiences in the snippets of text they left behind—were determined to touch the wild.

CREATING THE APPALACHIAN TRAIL

The ability to cope with nature directly—unshielded by the weakening wall of civilization—is one of the admitted needs of modern times.

—Benton MacKaye, "An Appalachian Trail: A Project in Regional Planning," Journal of the American Institute of Architects, *1921*

In 1921, the regional planner, socialist and dreamer Benton MacKaye published an essay in the *Journal of the American Institute of Architects* in which he proposed creating "an Appalachian Trail" that would extend from Mount Washington in New Hampshire to Mount Mitchell in North Carolina. In his youth, MacKaye was an avid hiker, often venturing into the nearby Green or White Mountains with friends or rambling around the more accommodating mountains of Massachusetts. As a Harvard-trained regional planner, he was very familiar with projects like the AMC's building of the trail network in the White Mountains, but perhaps the project that had the greatest impact on his thinking about trails and their role in American society was taking shape in Vermont, just north of the stomping grounds of his youth in Western Massachusetts. Begun a decade before MacKaye proposed the AT, the Green Mountain Club's Long Trail provided MacKaye with all the inspiration he needed for an even grander vision.

Ultimately covering 273 miles from the Massachusetts/Vermont border to Vermont's border with Canada just north of Jay Peak, the Long Trail began at a meeting of friends at the Van Ness Hotel in Burlington, Vermont, in

Benton MacKaye along the Appalachian Trail, 1930s. *Potomac Appalachian Trail Club Archives.*

March 1910. James Taylor, an educator and passionate promoter of economic development in the Green Mountain State, convinced his audience to create a hiking club that would be known as the Green Mountain Club with a singular purpose: to build a very long trail through Vermont's mountains, open to all hikers who wanted to access the summits of those mountains. An assistant principal at the Vermont Academy in Saxton's River, Taylor liked to take his students on long hikes in the forest but was frustrated by what he perceived, somewhat incorrectly, to be the lack of good hiking trails to the summits of Vermont's important peaks. In Taylor's view, having such a trail would make those peaks accessible to local hikers but would also draw more tourists to the state, helping to diversify its economy, which was largely based on agriculture, mining and lumbering. Although historians like to point out that there were plenty of trails to Vermont's peaks and that Taylor just wasn't aware of them, that didn't matter. What mattered was that his frustration over a *perceived* lack of good trails led to the creation of the country's first truly long-distance hiking trail, as opposed to the loop trails that were more the norm. The Long Trail was an audacious project both because of its length and because Vermont's forests and mountains posed very challenging terrain for trail builders. That audacity and the community-based, all-volunteer nature of the project helped the Long Trail become the inspiration for the Appalachian Trail.

As was true with the vast majority of America's outdoor clubs, the Green Mountain Club's early leaders were mostly members of the state's well-educated elite: judges, professors, high school principals, teachers, bankers, engineers and business owners—people who had the leisure time and the funds to spend their weekends hacking away at a trail and eventually maintaining it once it was complete. At the same time, those members of the elite knew how to get things done, how to work the levers of power in their community, how to negotiate with landowners for easements and how to advocate for the state to purchase land for a trail, and their work lives were not as unrelenting as a farmer's nor as exhausting as mining or lumbering. The members of the trail clubs who came together to create the Appalachian Trail had a similar socioeconomic profile for many of the same reasons. Building the Long Trail was a project confined to a relatively small group of hiking enthusiasts, and it would be a stretch to say that the idea of building the Long Trail was popular in Vermont. It's not so much that hiking was *unpopular* as it was that the average Vermonter just wasn't interested in hiking, much less the heavy labor of scouting, flagging, cutting, grading and then maintaining a trail through the difficult wilderness of Vermont's Green

Mountains. But to the middle-class founders of the GMC, getting into the woods to create something audacious like a 270-mile-long trail appealed to their pride and their sense of adventure. They wanted to do something big, and creating the Long Trail definitely qualified as big.

Work on the trail began the following year, and GMC volunteers managed to survey, flag, cut and grade the first twenty-nine miles of the trail from Camel's Hump to Smuggler's Notch, but the work had taken much longer than they anticipated. To speed things along, club leaders worked out a deal with the state forestry service to pay professional foresters to cut the trail for them. Through this cooperative arrangement, within eight years a little more than two hundred miles of the Long Trail had been completed, along with more than forty trail shelters for hikers to use. The last seventy or so miles took another ten years to complete, but when the work was done, the Long Trail was America's first truly long-distance hiking trail.

Americans have always been a restless people, and since the late nineteenth century, that restlessness has included a desire to pit man (or woman) against nature. Because the Long Trail was a *very long* trail, attempting to hike the whole thing in one go caught on fairly quickly as an idea among a small, hardy and dedicated group of hikers who aspired to do something difficult. As more and more hikers managed to make the trip between the Massachusetts/Vermont border and Canada, they even acquired a nickname: "End to Enders." Although the Green Mountain Club did not begin publishing the names of End to Enders until the 1940s, among the first of these hikers was one Irving D. Appleby of Roxboro, Massachusetts, who traversed the entire distance between Massachusetts and Canada in fourteen days. In other words, he didn't just hike it all—he hiked it *fast*. A newspaper story about his 1927 hike reported that he "[did] his own cooking and [slept] on the ground at night," as though these were truly remarkable achievements. His diet consisted mostly of cereal grains, raisins, sugar, bacon and hardtack, and like all backpackers of his day, he carried a short-handled axe on his belt so he could build a cooking fire. In the interview after his hike, Appleby lauded the GMC: "I cannot pay too high a tribute to their untiring efforts in keeping the trail open for the pleasure of vacationists."

But perhaps the most famous of the Long Trail's End to Enders were the so-called "Three Musketeers"—Hilda M. Kurth, Kathleen Norris and Catherine Robbins—who hiked the entire Long Trail in the summer of 1927. Like Appleby, they also packed light, carrying well under thirty pounds of gear and food in their Maine basket packs and rucksacks. James Taylor was wise enough to know that three young women hiking a difficult (and

The first three women to hike the Long Trail, 1927. *Appalachian Trail Conservancy Archives.*

still incomplete) trail through the mountains was a marketing opportunity for the Long Trail, and he made sure to make the most of it, telling just about anyone who would listen about their hike, especially newspapermen. Their success in reaching the Canadian border one month after they began resulted in national publicity for the Long Trail, including an article in the *New York Times*. While female long-distance hikers aren't news today, in 1927 the Three Musketeers made quite a splash. Their success set an important precedent in hiking clubs across the country, namely that women were just as able in the outdoors as men.

Benton MacKaye had been paying close attention to what was happening in Vermont, and the idea of creating a regional, as opposed to single-state, long-distance trail percolated in his mind for several years before the publication of his famous essay. It wasn't until 1921, following the suicide of his wife, Betty Stubbs, that MacKaye finally pulled his unformed ideas together into a more organized proposal. In his time of grief, his friend Horace Whitaker invited MacKaye to come to his estate in the mountains of New Jersey to rest and recuperate. While MacKaye was there, he wrote the article that appeared in the *Journal of the American Institute of Architects* after some considerable editing by Whitaker. In that essay, MacKaye laid out a vision rooted in his views about rural development, mental health and the value of time in nature to help people deal with what he called "the problem of living" in a modern industrial society. Drawing on his socialist ideals, MacKaye wanted workers in the big cities of the East Coast to be able to spend some time under the trees, to get some oxygen and some quiet back into their lives.

When his essay appeared, what really captured people's imagination was not solving the problem of living but rather the idea of a really long hiking trail. To MacKaye's surprise and pleasure, members of hiking clubs up and down the East Coast thought that it would be wonderful to build such a trail, and they started inviting MacKaye to visit and talk about his Appalachian Trail idea. It's a reasonable question to ask why the idea for a really long hiking trail would catch on so quickly when, at that moment, the Long Trail was the only example of such a trail. According to historian Sarah Mittlefehldt, "It was a culmination of these progressive era ideas where people were really starting to think about the interconnections between the hinterlands and the city and connections between all of the cities along the Eastern seaboard. A lot of historical figures get these big ideas when the timing is right and I really think it was it was all about the timing, I think he just kind of nailed it." MacKaye's clear and coherent vision landed among a group of trail clubs that were ready for a challenge, and what could be a bigger challenge than a two-thousand-mile-long trail?

Almost immediately, local trail clubs began building bits and pieces of the new trail, but by early 1925, it was clear to MacKaye and others that all the small-scale trail-building efforts underway needed to be coordinated. So, MacKaye did something his many years of government service had taught him how to do: he convened a meeting. But not just any meeting. The individuals MacKaye brought together in Washington, D.C., on March 2, 1925, were a who's who of the American conservation movement and federal agencies concerned with land conservation. Stephen Mather, the first director of the National Park Service, was there, as was Arthur Comey, the secretary of the New England Trail Conference. William Greeley, director of the U.S. Forest Service, was there, and so was William Welch, head of the Palisades Interstate Park Commission, who chaired the meeting. These were people of action, who knew how to get things done, with connections to money and the power of federal and state agencies. During the meeting, they decided to form what they called the Appalachian Trail Conference, which was a loosely organized confederation of various local trail clubs up and down the East Coast.

Benton MacKaye's original proposal for the Appalachian Trail, 1921. *Appalachian Trail Conservancy Archives.*

These clubs committed themselves to coordinating their activities and to completing the building of the two-thousand-mile trail. In a harbinger of what was to come in just a few years, they gave Benton MacKaye no role in managing the organization that he had called into being. It was apparent to all of them that MacKaye didn't have the managerial skill to run a sprawling organization like the Trail Conference. Instead, they gave him the task of continuing to promote the trail by giving lectures and writing stories for newspapers and magazines—things he was good at.

It didn't take long for the trail-building project to gather steam. Almost immediately, volunteers were out in the woods, marking off sections of the trail, organizing things, getting dirty and having fun. According to historian Larry Anderson, the trail project began at a propitious moment. The economy was booming, more and more people had cars to take them to the mountains for trail work and middle-class hikers had the leisure time to spend on the project. But what really made the project gather steam was the leadership of a young government lawyer named Myron Avery. Born in Lubec, Maine, as far east as you can travel and still be in the United States, Avery was twenty years younger than Benton MacKaye. They weren't just from different generations—they were from different worlds. Although they were both New Englanders and both held graduate degrees from Harvard, Avery was from a lower-middle-class family, and for him, higher education was a way to avoid a life working in one of the many sardine canning factories like the one his father managed or on a fishing boat. According to his biographer, Jeff Ryan, Avery learned the value of hard work in Lubec, but it "also taught him that he didn't want anything to do with living near a sardine factory." Instead, Avery spent his free time inland, hiking in the mountains and the wild forests of Maine, and the mountain he came to love best was Katahdin, Maine's highest peak.

What he *did* share with MacKaye was the desire to do something big, something he'd be known for. After graduating from Bowdoin College and then taking a law degree at Harvard, Avery moved to Washington, D.C., where he found a job as a government attorney. While settling into life in Washington, he joined a local hiking club called the Wildflower Preservation Society, which gave him his introduction to organized hiking. In 1927, Avery heard about the Appalachian Trail, and he knew he'd found the thing he'd been looking for. He convinced several of his friends in the Wildflower Preservation Society to form a new hiking club, one that would be devoted to helping build the AT, and they named their new club the Potomac Appalachian Trail Club (PATC). Like so many members of the trail-building clubs that appeared after 1925, the PATC members set about scouting and then building the Appalachian Trail in their area, which in their case meant north and south of the Potomac River.

Avery had the energy level of two humans, and right away he was out in the forest with other volunteers, hacking a route north and south from Linden, Virginia (where the trail crosses under Interstate 66 today). He also had a very strong personality. Before long, Avery was taking on more and more of a leadership role in the ATC, and eventually, he became that group's chairman in addition to being the president of the PATC. Avery was not easy to get along with; in fact, most people he worked with on the AT respected him but didn't like him much. He was abrasive, driven, exacting and often found insults where none existed—insults he felt bound to return twice over. When he died in 1952 at the age of fifty-two, the leader of one of the other trail clubs quipped that Avery had left two trails behind—the Appalachian

Myron Avery on the trail with his measuring wheel, 1935. *Appalachian Trail Conservancy Archives.*

Trail and a trail of bruised egos. But the Appalachian Trail hikers know today is the trail Avery insisted on. So many of the features of the trail that hikers recognize and depend on are part of the trail because Avery wouldn't have it any other way. The white blazes, trail shelters with their privies, signs with accurate mileages and many of the trail guides published by the ATC and the various clubs exist because Avery knew that hikers needed these things if they were going to have a good experience on the trail. In addition, the fundamental principles of trail location are a legacy of Avery's view of what the trail should be like. He wanted hikers, whether they were out for a few hours or a few days, to be challenged on their hike, but not so challenged that they couldn't make it, and that at the end of that challenge, there should be something rewarding—a beautiful overlook, a waterfall or an arresting geological formation—that served as a payoff for all their effort.

What Avery *didn't* care so much about was keeping the trail away from roads. He and his supporters within the ATC were much more interested in having a *completed* trail than they were in having a wilderness trail. What this meant for hikers was that when the trail clubs couldn't find a route through the mountains that worked for the trail, they simply routed the trail on rural roads and sometimes highways. In fact, when the Appalachian Trail was declared completed in 1937, it's likely that more than half of the entire

Albert Gordon, Dutch Roth, Carlos Campbell, Guy Frizzell, Myron Avery and Oliver Crowder on a hike from Newfound Gap to Deals Gap, Tennessee, 1931. *University of Tennessee Archives.*

"trail" was on a gravel or paved road. As late as the early 1980s, as much as one-third of the trail remained on roads, and it wasn't until after the U.S. Congress eventually appropriated enough funds to ramp up land acquisition for the trail corridor that the vast majority of the trail's route was moved off

roads and into the forest. While it might have been possible to create a much more wilderness-focused trail that was more isolated from roads and towns, that's not how the AT developed. Avery and his allies saw the trail as first and foremost a recreational resource, a place for hikers to go and experience nature. They wanted that resource to be a continuous trail from Maine to Georgia because a two-thousand-mile-long trail would be appealing to hikers, if only because it was so grandiose. If sections of that trail were on roads or wove back and forth across roads, so be it. Having the trail come close to or through towns also had the advantage of providing hikers with places to purchase supplies before their hikes, to have a meal after a hike or to spend the night in a home or a hotel. The Appalachian Trail hikers know today still crisscrosses roads and still comes close to or through towns, and the boom in long-distance hiking on the trail is possible for those very reasons. Long-distance hikers must resupply every five to seven days, so being able to walk into a town to visit a store or the local post office to pick up a supply box is essential to being able to hike for more than a week on the trail.

If Benton MacKaye had had his way in the 1930s, that kind of long-distance hiking experience would not have been possible. MacKaye saw the AT not so much as a recreational resource but as a chance for people to experience *wilderness*. He thoroughly objected to routing the trail anywhere near a road, except at trailheads, much less crisscrossing back and forth across roads as it does in places like Shenandoah National Park or along the Blue Ridge Parkway. In 1934, MacKaye wrote that roads such as Skyline Drive "violate the wilderness solitude, not merely here and there, but throughout their whole length." MacKaye's insistence that the Appalachian Trail should be first and foremost a wilderness trail led to a dispute with Avery in 1935 centered on the route of the AT in Shenandoah National Park, a dispute that permanently fractured their relationship. After a bitter exchange of letters over this issue, the two men never spoke again. MacKaye exiled himself from the project, going off to help found the Wilderness Society with several other preservationists, and Avery brought the trail to its first completion in 1937 when a Civilian Conservation Corps (CCC) crew built the final missing segment in Maine. The tension at the center of this dispute—was the Appalachian Trail a wilderness trail or a recreational trail—remains. The National Park Service and the ATC are constantly trying to balance their desire to have the hiking experience be as wild as possible while still keeping the trail as accessible as possible, but fortunately, road walking is mostly a thing of the past.

One of Avery's solutions for making the trail more accessible to more people was to propose the building of a chain of shelters up and down the trail. In his 1937 report to the ATC's annual meeting in Gatlinburg, Avery wrote:

> *The Trail project has reached a stage now where careful thought should be given to its better utilization and protection. To this end we have two courses of action which we believe to be constructive. The first is the matter of*

> *appurtenances. It is elementary to require elaboration, that the Appalachian Trail system requires a system of accommodations along its route. In the ideal, this should be dual system. Shelters for those who wish to camp. Wherever possible, listed available public accommodations for those who prefer to expend their energy other than in carrying equipment.*

Some accommodations already existed, like the AMC's hut system and the Green Mountain Club's shelters along the Long Trail (which the AT shared for more than one hundred miles) in Maine. Hikers could stay at sporting camps located at reasonable intervals all along the trail's route. Hikers on the AT in Maine might be surprised to realize that in the trail's earliest decades, hiking the trail there was much more of a pleasant jaunt between fishing and hunting camps that served delicious meals at the end of one day and the start of the next than it was a slog through bogs and over steep, flinty ridges as it is today. For the rest of the trail, Avery exhorted the trail clubs to begin building rustic shelters along the trail at conveniently spaced intervals. The distance between the shelters should not be so great that the average hiker would struggle to get from one to the next in a day. Each should have a consistent water source, each should include a nearby privy and each should have a fire pit both for cooking and for throwing warmth into the open-fronted shelters at night. If possible, each shelter should afford hikers a pleasant view of the mountains, a nearby lake or stream or something equally pleasing for the end of their day's effort.

The AMC's Lakes of the Clouds Hut, 1937. Photographer unknown.

The building of a chain of shelters would, in many ways, be as difficult or even more difficult than scouting, building and marking a trail through the forest. Lumber for flooring and roofs had to be carried to building sites, trees had to be cut and peeled for the walls, bunk beds had to be carried in or built (many of the early shelters had bunks) and roofing material, paint, nails and other necessary items also had to be carried to the building sites. Given how much work shelter construction was going to be, representatives of several of the trail clubs asked whether the shelters might therefore be reserved for the use of club members. Avery and Ed Ballard from the National Park Service (also a proponent of building a chain of shelters) answered with a resounding "No." The Appalachian Trail, they said, was a trail for the American people, not for the exclusive or semi-exclusive use of trail club members, so the shelters would be open to all hikers. Although this decision seemed not especially consequential at the time, it had profound implications for the later development of the AT. Had the shelters been reserved for those who built and maintained them, then the Appalachian Trail would have been a much more private endeavor. It likely would not have become the public recreational resource it is today, and it's a reasonable question whether it would have survived at all had it been a more exclusive place. Over time, as the trail became more and more popular with backpackers, the ATC and the trail clubs instituted a policy designating the shelters as first of all for the use of long-distance hikers. But what, exactly, "long-distance hiker" means has never been defined, leading to a fair amount of misperception on the trail in the past several decades. Many thru hikers believe that the shelters are reserved for them, and some can be testy or impolite with other backpackers who might be using the shelters. At no time have the shelters been reserved for those attempting a thru hike. They remain, as Avery insisted in 1937, resources for the general hiking public, not a small segment of the hiking community.

Because building the shelters in the 1930s, 1940s and 1950s was a difficult task for the trail clubs, they often chose to locate shelters either near roads or fire roads. This proximity to roads also made it easier to bring building materials to the site by truck or jeep. As we will see in the "Trail Shelters" chapter, the decision to locate so many of the shelters near roadways had a profound impact on what happened at those shelters once backpacking and wilderness hiking took off in the 1960s and 1970s. The other issue the trail clubs faced in the building out of a shelter chain was that most of the original Appalachian Trail was located on private land. Building a permanent structure on someone else's land required careful negotiation

Hikers at the Deep Gap Shelter, Georgia, 1935. *Appalachian Trail Conservancy Archives.*

with landowners and much more formal agreements than the handshake or sometimes not very formal written agreements the local trail clubs reached with landowners regarding easements for the trail to cross their land. After the passage of the National Trails Systems Act in 1968, landowners began to realize that the Appalachian Trail was about to become a national park, which might mean that they would lose control of their property. Some of those landowners began canceling their easements for the trail and demanding the removal of the trail shelters. In some cases, the local trail clubs had to beg to be allowed to remove a shelter so that it could be reassembled elsewhere, and in at least one example I found in the archives, a landowner in Pennsylvania simply canceled his easement for the AT and turned the trail shelter on his land into a mower shed, refusing all entreaties from the local club regarding the disassembly of the structure.

Because the chain of trail shelters *was* built, the Appalachian Trail became a much more accessible trail for the average hiker. The shelters were destinations that could be planned around. Even if there was no space inside, there were tenting areas nearby, there was usually a consistent water source and there was almost always (but not always) a privy. Hikers who wanted more isolation in the forest could camp elsewhere along the trail, but for those who wanted both a wilderness experience and a social experience, the more than 250 trail shelters eventually built along the AT provided that social opportunity. The shelters became a place to meet other hikers, a place to exchange ideas and experiences and a place for bonding in the face of adverse conditions along the trail. The shelter registers are filled with examples of hikers sharing food, stories, water and space when the weather turned foul or dangerous. They were places to observe wildlife—sometimes wildlife that came too close in search of goodies in hikers' packs—and they were places to sit around a fire and chat, sing or just rest. The attractiveness of the shelters as destinations had the collateral benefit of concentrating human impact in a relatively small number of places along the trail, something that has mattered a great deal more in the past thirty years or so as the number of backpackers continues to grow.

The trail shelters are popular for all these reasons, but perhaps one of the most important reasons why hikers like them so much is that they mediate between the hiker and the wild. A three-sided trail shelter doesn't prevent a skunk, a bear or a mouse from crawling inside to see if you brought anything that might taste good. Snakes, wasps and other less desirable denizens of the forest also like to spend time in the shelters. But when a hiker is inside, even if one wall is just a big opening, there is the illusion of safety, the sense that from the vantage point of the interior of that structure, wildlife and wild weather can be observed safely. At the same time, because the shelters are (mostly) open to the world, hikers are close to the wild nature they came to see on their hike. If the shelters had been built as cabins with four walls, there just wouldn't be the same immediacy, the same proximity with the natural world.

> *Just dropped in to enjoy a fine and gorgeous autumn day. Sunny and 50 degrees. Just about perfect. Hope this note finds those reading it as peaceful as I am right now.*
>
> —*Maryland, 2000*

By the end of the 1950s, the Appalachian Trail had become the trail first envisioned by Benton MacKaye and then driven to completion by the ATC and the local trail clubs. The trail was a continuous footpath from Maine to Georgia, albeit with a lot of road walking. The chain of shelters was more or less completed, although there remained a few gaps longer than fifteen miles between shelters. The trail was well marked, and signs stood at most major and even minor intersections. Hikers were starting to walk longer distances on the trail than ever before, and by 1960, almost twenty had hiked the entire trail, either in sections or all in one season. The growing prosperity of America in the aftermath of World War II and the rapid increase in automobile ownership meant that more and more casual hikers were coming to the AT for a few hours or perhaps a day or two. While MacKaye and Avery certainly didn't agree on what kind of trail the Appalachian Trail should be, they both wanted it to become the kind of trail it was turning into—a place where thousands of hikers could get away from their city lives and spend some time just being in nature.

THE FIRST DECADES

The pleasure of walking, or rather of hiking, comes from the utter sense of freedom incident to getting away from crowded cities and equally crowded highways, from escaping the daily grind over desk or bench, in office, school, or shop, and discovering the beauties and peace of the forest primeval.

—Roy Ozmer, "Do You Want to Walk 2,000 Miles?,"
Atlanta Constitution, *September 16, 1928*

When the Appalachian Trail began to take shape after the first meeting of the Appalachian Trail Conference in 1925, it looked very little like the trail we know today, with a few notable exceptions. The section of the AT routed along the Appalachian Mountain Club's trails in the White Mountains was on a collection of well-established trails that looked and felt much like the current version of the trail, and many of those early sections in the Whites are still part of the AT today. The same was true in the Green Mountains of Vermont, where the Appalachian Trail took advantage of the preexisting Long Trail for about one hundred miles. In New York, Connecticut, Massachusetts, New Jersey, Pennsylvania and Maryland, there were bits and pieces of existing trails that the planners of the AT could take advantage of, such as a few sections in Bear Mountain State Park, but otherwise, a two-thousand-mile trail largely had to be constructed from scratch.

The early trail builders were in a hurry. Once they decided to build a trail from Maine to Georgia, they wanted the project done as quickly as possible, which meant they looked for any way they could find to speed things up. One of the fastest ways to do that was to use old roads in the mountains that had fallen into disuse or completely out of use decades earlier. Those roads were old, sometimes more than one hundred years old, and many were located on routes first created by Indigenous peoples of the Appalachian Mountains. Because Indigenous trail makers chose routes that were practical, easy to follow and took full advantage of the contours of the terrain, their older paths were just too tempting to pass up when European settlers began building their own transportation network. What was lost in the creation of that network was the deep connection between Native peoples and the geography their trails traversed. Europeans wanted routes that got from one place to another in an efficient way. For Indigenous people, geography and memory are deeply intertwined, and the ways that they speak about the land in their own languages reinforce those connections. Place names along Indigenous paths told stories that connected the present with the past and future. Settler roads and trails were just roads and trails.

All along the Appalachian Trail today, it is still easy to see where the trail took advantage of abandoned mountain roads. The trail is wider; you can often see two ruts where the wheels of carts, trucks and cars compacted the soil; and in many places, the sides of the trail are raised and often lined with stones removed by road builders to smooth out the roadbed. Sometimes there are even stone walls, the labor of many years, supporting the roadbed and keeping it more or less level. Those remnants of past mountain settlements are everywhere along the AT and give hikers a sense not only for the most recent occupation of those mountains by farmers and hunters but also of lives lived in places where farming was challenging, where peoples' lives were governed by seasons, by weather, by the slope of the land and the presence or lack of game in the forests. In addition to hiking along those old roadbeds, AT hikers today pass by stone chimneys, seemingly alone in the forest, and barely visible paths leading to a few headstones, some tended by relatives who still remember their ancestors and others broken, toppled or long overgrown by vines. Appalachian families often planted trees in and around their family cemeteries and then periwinkle around the headstones. The trees were there to provide shade, and the periwinkle's job was to crowd out all other plant growth, making the cemetery easier to maintain. The trees, often cedars, are large now or dead, broken and fallen, but you can often see a large area of periwinkle off in the forest, seemingly there for no reason. If you do, the odds are good that a cemetery or the foundations of a home lie beneath the undergrowth. Those old cemeteries don't always have headstones, but if you look carefully, you can sometimes see a few depressions in the ground marking the locations of long-forgotten graves. Appalachian Trail hikers can also see what seem like randomly placed piles of stones, sometimes as high as a grown person's chest, right next to the trail. If you look carefully, you may see a large, flat stone somewhere in the middle of that pile, usually on the far side, facing away from the trail. That flat stone is the lintel from an old hearth, and the rock pile is what archaeologists call a chimney fall, the remnant of the old chimney offering evidence that a home once stood there. By our lights today, having your house right up against a trail or a road seems, well, not very private. But in the nineteenth and early twentieth centuries, it was a practical choice.

The landscapes the trail passed through in its earliest days were also places of great ecological sadness. Before 1920, the dominant tree species in the Appalachian Mountains, at least as far north as Vermont, was the American chestnut. Billions and billions of chestnut trees carpeted those mountains and were an essential component of the natural and human ecosystems. Chestnut trees were often huge—among the largest trees in North America. Photographs in the archives of the trail clubs show members standing or leaning against the boles of chestnut trees in groups of four or five, and the humans don't blot out the entire trunk. But by the time hikers began walking on the Appalachian Trail, almost all those billions of trees were dead, killed off by a fungus brought to the United States decades earlier from Asia.

The death of all those billions of trees was devastating to the natural ecosystem and the mountain economy, causing thousands of Appalachian residents to pull up stakes and move. Without the trees that were central to their local economy, staying in the mountains just no longer made sense. But the tragedy of the American chestnut was, in some ways, a boon to those building the Appalachian Trail. They were able to harvest the trunks of the dead trees to build trail shelters, some of which still stand today. They also used the trunks and branches to build bridges over streams and for erosion control along the trail. Sadly, the death of the American chestnut tree was just one of several afflictions that have descended on the trees of the Appalachian Mountains since hikers first began their journeys north and south along the trail. In the 1970s *Lymantria dispar dispar* (the spongy moth) began spreading in the forests of Appalachia, and their larvae have defoliated large swaths of the mountains traversed by the trail. In the 1960s, *Adelges tsugae* (the hemlock woolly adelgid) began wreaking destruction on the hemlock forests of North America. As the climate warms, the spread of the wooly adelgid has only accelerated. Along the AT,

the devastation caused by the adelgid is most apparent in the Great Smoky Mountains National Park and in Vermont, where the hemlock forests are in substantial danger of succumbing to this pest. Now, in the 2020s, *Agrilus planipennis* (the emerald ash borer) is wiping out the ash trees up and down the spine of the Appalachians. Trail and shelter maintainers are hard-pressed to keep up with the deaths of these trees, dropping the ones that pose hazards to hikers or trail structures and using the smaller trunks as water bars and check dams where stones aren't readily available. A century of tree death due to introduced pathogens and pests and heavy logging in some areas has meant that the forests of the Appalachian Mountains look very little like the forests AT hikers passed through in the trail's first decades. If a similar pest or blight turns up to take out the tulip poplar and the various species of oak along the trail, there may be very few large trees left for hikers to enjoy and for the many forest species to use for their own life purposes.

The trees weren't the only things to pass from the story of the trail. By the time the ATC and the trail clubs began laying out the Appalachian Trail, the mountains of Appalachia were depopulating. The death of the chestnut tree caused significant damage to the mountain economy, but it wasn't the only blow the mountain people had to absorb. Except in Pennsylvania, the Appalachian Trail does not pass through any of the coal-producing regions of Appalachia, but it did traverse areas where small-scale mining for copper, iron, lead, zinc and manganese happened. Almost all these mines were small-scale operations worked by local miners who lived in mountain communities nearby. By the 1920s, those small mines were largely depleted or had been forced out of business by much larger and more economical mineral strikes in the Upper Midwest and in the western mountain ranges. Towns like Rausch Gap, Pennsylvania, simply died and began to decay back into the forest. Mountain residents who depended on the mines for jobs and the towns for supplies had no choice but to move away. In many ways, the Great Depression was just the final body blow to many mountain communities, forcing more and more people to abandon the way of life their families had known for generations. In addition, the creation of the Great Smoky Mountains National Park and Shenandoah National Park resulted in thousands of mountain residents being forced

Smoky Mountains Hiking Club members enjoying the big chestnut tree stop, Tennessee, 1932. *University of Tennessee Archives.*

from their land and their homes by local and state governments to make way for the two new national parks.

As property owners began to abandon their farms and fields, the U.S. Forest Service embarked on an aggressive campaign of land acquisition that resulted in substantial growth in several of the national forests now home to the AT. In the two new national parks, the homes, the barns, the sheds, the fences and the stone walls made by mountain residents were removed to supposedly return the mountains to some imagined pre-settler state of nature, but the forest service tended to leave those structures in place, letting them simply rot back into the forests. In the earliest days of the Appalachian Trail, before the chain of trail shelters began to take shape, hikers were advised to make use of the properties abandoned by Appalachian farm families. The first guidebooks offer lots of advice about camping in an "abandoned barn" or in an "abandoned house." Springs and wells were often to be found at those old homesites, so hikers were directed there for water. What is *not* evident in either the early trail guides or in the archives of the ATC and the trail clubs is any sense of loss or poignancy connected to the abandoned farms that spoke so eloquently to the failed hopes of mountain families. Instead, those abandoned farms were just resources, providing easily accessed (and free) accommodations for hikers along the trail. Early AT hikers definitely took full advantage of those free lodgings.

The scattered accounts of hikes from the 1930s and the 1940s describe staying in such homes, although not always as restfully as one might have hoped. For example, in 1935, two hikers stopped in one such abandoned house near Ashby Gap in Northern Virginia. They had been hiking in nothing but rain for several days, so the prospect of sleeping dry under a roof was too enticing to pass up. But it didn't turn out well:

> *As it has started to rain again we have moved into the Presidential Suite on the second floor. This damn place is so full of rats that it sounds like a barn dance in the attic. The first floor is used as a rendezvous for about 20 cows…they're having a terrific time. No manners whatsoever.…Am writing this by candlelight. Those damn rats are just raising the roof. Sounds like a fight. It's too bad we can't have a little harmony here. You can't scare the bloody scoundrels by stomping on the floor. I sure hope they don't try to get personal tonight.*

This lack of interest, or at least the lack of formal recognition of the fate of mountain families, is perhaps not all that surprising. The people who came to the mountains to build the Appalachian Trail *came to* the mountains. Most were not *from* the mountains, and at that moment in American history, journalists, writers, politicians and college professors had been going out of their way to cast the people of Appalachia as backward, uneducated, inbred, inferior and culturally and educationally deprived. They were, to put it bluntly, a convenient "other" against which other Americans could measure themselves. Given that the people who became enthralled with the notion of an Appalachian Trail were residents of the urban and suburban areas of the East Coast, it's no wonder that when Appalachian people were being described in such pejorative terms, the early trail volunteers often saw mountain residents in this way.

Not everyone did, of course, but the exceptions stand out in the archives. Frank Schairer, one of the founders of the Potomac Appalachian Trail Club in Washington, D.C., was one of those exceptions. A prominent physicist working at the Carnegie Institution Geophysical Laboratory, Schairer built strong relationships with the mountain communities in what was soon to become Shenandoah National Park. He visited mountain residents in their homes, drank moonshine and homemade brandy with them, sang and danced with them and just generally became their friend, so much so that he was known to many in those communities simply as "Dr. Frank." Similarly, one of the most important of the ATC's trail scouts in Western North Carolina and East Tennessee was the Asheville-based photographer George Masa, an immigrant from Japan who spoke thickly accented English and was one of the founders of the Carolina Mountain Club. Masa had an almost preternatural ability to drive his battered car up into steeply sloped mountain coves to visit with often elderly farmers, sitting on their front porches and discussing in detail the stories behind the naming of this or that peak. At a time when many peaks in the eastern mountains had no official name or might have several competing names, ATC Chairman Myron Avery was especially hell-bent on publishing trail guides that were *correct*. To that end, he sent Masa again and again up into the mountains to try to get the most correct version of the name of a particular peak. I've often wondered what those elderly mountain residents made of Masa with his dark skin, his awkward English and his love for listening to their stories.

When the early trail builders couldn't use abandoned or little-used mountain roads—or any existing trails—they had two choices. The first and much more difficult and labor-intensive choice was to recruit volunteer trail scouts or hire people employed by local state and/or federal agencies, usually forest services, to plot out routes over mountain peaks, down through saddles and across rivers. This work required not only a surveyor's eye but also experience routing paths through often difficult and very steep terrain. Those trail scouts would often flag a route by chopping marks in tree bark as they passed, and then trail-building crews would follow along after them over months or years and begin laying down the actual trail. That initial work was often mostly about clearing vegetation—small trees, cat briars and other kinds of undergrowth—to make a path hikers could follow. It was very labor intensive, and a really good weekend of trail clearing might result in a mile or perhaps as many as three miles of trail being cleared. Because the early trail builders were weekend warriors, progress on what might be called virgin trail was understandably slow, which helps to explain why in the earliest days of the Appalachian Trail, the ATC and the clubs relied so heavily on old mountain roads or preexisting paths. The exception, of course, was getting the trail to peaks and scenic overlooks. Those old roads almost never reached a mountain peak and only rarely came close to a spot that might work as a scenic overlook. They were practical roads, leading to farms, barns and pastures from the larger road network down below. They weren't laid out to be scenic. If the AT was going to be a trail with beautiful views—the reward for a difficult hike to a summit—trail builders were going to have to lay out and cut paths to those spots no matter what.

Of course, most of the land that the early trail crossed was private land, owned either by farmers or corporations—mostly mining and timber companies. If the farmer had abandoned his land, the early trail builders just routed the AT across that property without any sort of formal agreement. If the farmer was still on his land or if the land belonged to a corporation, then the clubs and the ATC had to arrange an easement for the trail, typically for the princely sum of one dollar per year. Only rarely does one find in the archives examples of landowners refusing to allow the AT to cross their property in the 1930s or the 1940s. It was only after the Second World War, when private land began to pass into the hands of a new generation of owners, many of whom had no prior connection to the land or the Appalachian Trail (or hiking), that the clubs began to see their easements canceled and the trail pushed off its original route. To the average hiker, though, this was all opaque. Those hikers purchased a trail guide and followed the route in the guide, oblivious to the ownership of the land they walked on or of any easements or land use agreements that might have been negotiated by the local trail club.

When no mountain roads were available to use, or when a local landowner balked at allowing the trail to cross their property, the ATC and the clubs

Hikers on the Bear Mountain Bridge, circa 1980. *Appalachian Trail Conservancy Archives.*

resorted to just using roads, gravel or paved, that got hikers from Point A to Point B along the trail's route. Of course, roads are still a significant part of the Appalachian Trail today, but for some very practical reasons. Between Georgia and Maine, the AT crosses an uncounted number of rivers and streams. Most of those waterways can be forded by hikers, and in the early days of the trail, that's just what they did. But some rivers—such as the New, the James, the Potomac, the Susquehanna and the Hudson—could only be crossed on a bridge, which meant and still means a highway or railroad bridge, except in the case of the James, where the James River Footbridge (named for hiker and trail volunteer Bill Foot) opened in 2000. Many other smaller rivers could also only be crossed conveniently on highway or road bridges, so the volunteers laying out the trail took advantage of those bridges by bringing the trail down to a road at either end of a bridge. In Maine, the Kennebec River was also dangerous to cross. At first, hikers had two choices: they could hike miles out of their way to a bridge, and then miles back, or they could hope that someone living near the river could help. In 1951, a young hiker from Ohio named Bill Hall described the crossing this way:

> *The Kennebec River is wide and swift, with an amber color and stone bottom. It has a current like a millrace and is just as unpredictable. Square in our path, it winds across the state of Maine and dares any but the most skillful boatman to cross it. Now it's no feat to cross a river—even a tempestuous one like the Kennebec—with paddles or oars or a motor. But boats on the Kennebec are poled across and as I soon learned, it takes a bit of skill.*

Hall and his friend made it across, but about two hundred yards downstream from where they had planned to land. Eventually, the ATC and the Maine club arranged to have a canoe available for hikers that could be hauled back and forth across the Kennebec with a rope. These days, that canoe crossing is a manned canoe ferry during peak hiking season.

Until fairly recently, Appalachian Trail hikers also spent a lot of time strolling through farm fields. There are still some sections of the trail in pastures or, in the case of the Carlisle Valley in Pennsylvania, through some long stretches of cornfields. But in the 1930s and the 1940s, far more of the AT was still in open fields. Over time, as federal and state agencies began acquiring that farmland to add to the system of national forests and national parks, more and more trees began to fill in those old pastures, hayfields and paddocks. Federal programs helped with the reforesting of the mountains along the trail. One of the most important activities of the enrollees in the

Civilian Conservation Corps was the planting of trees, and AT hikers have those enrollees to thank for many of what are now mature forests along the Appalachian Trail's route.

These days, the Appalachian Trail can be a pretty crowded place, especially during the peak hiking season from early spring to late autumn. But in the early decades of the trail's existence, the AT was anything but crowded. It was, for instance, possible to hike from Harpers Ferry to Skyland in Shenandoah National Park in the late 1930s and meet no other hikers or to hike the length of the trail in the Smokies in the summer during the early 1940s and run into just six other hikers. The ferryman who took hikers across the New River in those early decades told a group of hikers in the late 1930s that he had put no more than five hikers across the river in the past twelve months. Of course, there were plenty of places along the AT in those early decades that saw a fair amount of foot traffic, but those were mostly spots like Kuwohi (formerly Clingmans Dome) or the summit of Mount Washington, which also had roads to the summit and were popular with day-trippers.

The trail in those early days could amaze hikers with its natural beauty. As one hiker wrote in 1939 after a long hike through the southern stretches of the trail:

> *One outstanding delight of the trip to all of us, possibly because it was so unexpected, was the magnificent oak forest with huge trees and grassy park-like floor, through which the trail runs with few breaks from a few miles south of Newfound Gap to about Rocky Knob Shelter in Georgia. None of us had ever seen anything like this before. Another constant pleasure was the wildflowers, whose profusion and varieties seemed to surpass those of the more northerly portions of the trail.*

Those early hikers also had a lot to say about the wildlife they encountered along the way. While bears were not nearly as common along the AT in its early years, they were not altogether absent and were more than willing to try entering trail shelters in search of food in hikers' packs. More common, though, were porcupines and skunks, both of which show up again and again in hiker commentary about wildlife found at the shelters:

> *Spent a peaceful night here. We were visited early in the morning by a hungry skunk looking for food. He or she made the rounds sniffing each of us and finally wound up eating our bread.*
>
> —*Georgia, 1951*

Skunks were (and remain) especially persistent when they scented something edible in a hiker's pack. Bear boxes and bear poles didn't exist at the shelters in those early decades, and I only found a few mentions in the archives of hanging a bag to keep it away from bears. Of course, mice and snakes show up quite often in hiker accounts, and although mountain lions have been extinct on the East Coast for many decades, in the trail's early days there were still a few to be found in isolated stretches of the trail along the North Carolina/Tennessee border, in Southwest Virginia and in Maine. But by the end of the Second World War, mountain lions were gone from the East, having been hunted to local extinction.

Trail maintenance was highly variable in those early decades and almost nonexistent during the Second World War. To the best of their ability, local trail clubs endeavored to keep their sections of the trail open, but hikers very often encountered what one hiker in the early 1950s described as a lot of "growed over trail." Blowdowns during winter storms have been the bane of the trail maintainer since the Appalachian Trail began, and in the early decades of the trail's existence, the removal of those blowdowns required the use of axes or handsaws. The modern gas-powered chainsaw that we are so familiar with didn't go into mass distribution in the United States until after the Second World War, so maintainers had to remove those blowdowns using human-powered tools—a much slower and more labor-intensive process. In 1938, the "Great New England Hurricane" crossed Long Island Sound and roared across southern New England and up into Vermont, killing more than 650 people and knocking down an estimated 2 billion trees in the Northeast. Long sections of the newly completed Appalachian Trail were blocked for years by the storm damage. Likewise, in August 1940, a major hurricane crossed the Carolinas and dumped its remaining moisture in Western North Carolina, East Tennessee and Southwest Virginia. While its devastation was not nearly as great as the storm two years earlier in New England, the 1940 storm also did major damage to the AT, and hikers had to avoid certain sections for more than a year until maintainers could clear all the downed trees. In 2024, Hurricane Helene wrecked similar devastation on the trail from Georgia into Southern Virginia.

Mostly, though, hikers on the AT before the Second World War found a well-marked and reasonably well-maintained trail to walk on, thanks to the efforts of countless trail club volunteers and a much more limited number of workers with the U.S. Forest Service, the CCC and the National Park Service. Trees, rocks and fence posts were blazed with the white rectangle so familiar to AT hikers today or with small tin markers, rock cairns led the way

Potomac Appalachian Trail Club members on the trail in southern Pennsylvania, circa 1938. *Potomac Appalachian Trail Club Archives.*

across open pastures and stiles built by club members helped hikers across cattle fences. The trail was mostly well graded, and while it did not have all the stone and log stairs one finds today, or the erosion control bars or the steppingstones to help hikers cross creeks and streams—much less all those bridges over creeks and streams—it was easily navigable by most hikers in most stretches.

In 1925 or 1935, or even until the late 1950s, when people went to hike on the Appalachian Trail, they most often went in groups—sometimes very large groups. And to get to a trailhead, they took trains, trolleys, buses and, increasingly, cars. Cars are efficient ways to get small numbers of people to the trail, but when your group counted twenty or more, that meant four, five or even six vehicles—and parking areas were almost unknown along the trail in its first decades. If hikers were members of trail clubs, Boy or Girl Scout troops, the YMCA or YWCA or church groups, they very often traveled to the trail either on a train from whichever big city they lived in—Boston, New York, Philadelphia, Washington, D.C., Asheville, Knoxville or Atlanta—or they went in a bus hired specifically to drop them off at the beginning of their hike and pick them up at the end of the day. The archives contain many photographs and even some grainy silent film of large numbers of hikers piling out of a chartered bus to hit the trail wearing clothes that can sometimes seem outlandish by today's standards: women wearing jodhpurs and men in vests, ties and homburg hats but all of them sporting proper hiking shoes or boots. Those large group hikes were often very well-planned events, with a stop at a picnic ground, a peak or a stream for lunch, and if the group stopped at a picnic ground, there might also be square dancing.

Dinner was often at a restaurant somewhere along the road back home, and local residents and business owners certainly appreciated the custom of large groups of hikers. Those early hikers could be a novelty in some of those rural communities though. Local residents were often fascinated by the very idea that someone would hire a bus and ride an hour or three to get to the mountains just to walk uphill. If those folks were backpackers with forty pounds or more on their back, well, that could seem downright odd. But it didn't take long for local residents to realize that the existence of the Appalachian Trail meant that more and more hikers would be coming each year and that this meant economic opportunity in depressed rural

Hikers hitting the trail in West Virginia, 1936. *Potomac Appalachian Trail Club Archives.*

communities (especially during the Great Depression). In those Depression years, rural communities were used to the sight of vagabonds, mostly men, wandering the roads in search of work, food and shelter, and oral histories of those days contain many stories of those wanderers coming to the door of a farmhouse in the evening looking for a meal or the chance to sleep in a barn.

But these hiking vagabonds were a different sort. They had enough money to pay for a bus, they could afford to eat in the local restaurant and they dressed well. And the backpackers, the ones who were out on the trail for several nights, would sometimes pay for a night and a meal at the home of a farm family. The old trail guides offer lots of advice (and telephone numbers) detailing how to get in touch with those who were willing to take in boarders, some of whom would even come and pick hikers up at a road crossing if that could be arranged in advance. Today, hikers would call it trail magic if a family along the trail offered them a place to sleep, shower and wash their clothes. In the 1930s, some families sometimes did so for free, but more often than not, they expected to be paid a nominal amount. In his account of his 1951 thru hike, Gene Espy told of several occasions where he had dinner with a farm family who refused to let him pay, so when no one was watching he would slip a dollar bill under the placemat and then mosey on up the trail. In one case, a family saved him from spending the night in a hailstorm:

> *The Eller family was exceptionally kind to me. They took me in, fed me supper, built a fire in the open fireplace so I could dry my clothes. When bedtime came, they let me sleep on a cot in the attic. I was awakened in the night by the loud rat-a-tat sound of hail pounding the tin roof a few inches above my head....After a good breakfast with these fine people I returned to the trail.*

The shelter registers offer example after example of hikers letting those who came after them know that farmer X would sell them a quart of milk or a dozen eggs or that farmer Y sold apple brandy. These were economic transactions, not trail magic, although it certainly would have been a bit magical to be able to purchase some fresh milk, eggs, cheese or brandy en route to a trail shelter and have a delicious meal cooked over the fire that night followed by some strong drink. In ways no one had anticipated when the ATC first met in 1925, the trail had quickly become deeply intertwined with the rural economies it passed through. For early AT hikers, this was a unique opportunity to connect, or in some cases reconnect, with rural

Americans who lived lives increasingly separate from the lives of those in urban areas. Well into the late twentieth century, hikers were still finding this sort of hospitality along the trail. For example, in the 1980s, one hiking guide advised, "Mr. Irwin (or is it Erwin?) allows hikers to sometimes stay in the large clean upstairs of his garage at 55 E. Main Street."

At a time of rapid urbanization and rural depopulation, the connections hikers made with local residents and vice-versa meant that hikers came away with a fuller understanding of the lives of rural Americans, and mountain residents came to know "city folk" as more than just ideas and stereotypes. These many connections are also reminders that in its early decades, long stretches of the AT were not remotely what we would call "wild." Benton MacKaye had wanted the trail to be easily accessible to the urban working classes, and while the workers of the cities didn't seem to spend a lot of time out on the trail, middle-class people did. Because the trail was often so close to those cities, in some places within a drive of less than an hour, and because it often followed roads or crossed cow pastures, early hikers were much more likely to come into direct contact with rural residents than they are today. These days, the trail is more removed from settled spaces and so hikers can, if they want, go days without encountering anyone who lives near the trail, except perhaps at a road crossing. But the trail always brings them back to a road or a town, and it is in those towns that connections, some brief, some lasting, are made. The planners of the Appalachian Trail didn't imagine the trail as a vehicle for cultural exchange, but that is exactly what it turned out to be.

WHAT THEY CARRIED

The loaded pack [without food or water], *with tent, for an eight-day trip other than in winter, should not exceed 35 lbs. for a man or 30 lbs. for a woman, and it is better if it is five lbs. lighter.*

—Jean Stephenson writing in the Appalachian Trailway News, *1955*

When the Appalachian Trail began, hiking and camping in the backcountry was not a complete novelty, but just like today, these activities remained a sport limited to those who craved a bit more adventure than the average American. Hunters, trappers and explorers had been going into the wild since Europeans arrived in North America, and a market slowly grew up around those adventurers to provide them with the gear they might need for their trips. But those trips were often quite different from what we might think of today as overnights in the wilderness. There were certainly lone hikers, or those who went in pairs or very small groups, but it was much more common for hikers to hit the trail in very large groups—sometimes as many as twenty to thirty people—even on overnight hikes requiring camping out. To use today's jargon for what many of those large group overnight trips were like, we might call what they did "slack packing," meaning they carried only what they needed to have with them while they were walking, while other members of their group set up camp at a destination, pitching the tents, setting up a camp kitchen and sometimes clearing a space for square dancing. All that gear and food arrived in cars and trucks, which were parked somewhere near the endpoint of the group's hike.

By the time the Appalachian Trail appeared on maps of the Eastern mountains, a robust market in hiking and camping gear already existed. Many of those early gear suppliers—such as Fiala Outfits, the U.S. Bobbin & Shuttle Company, C.C. Filson or Leibold and Company—are long gone or, like Abercrombie & Fitch, have gone into other lines of business than supplying gear to adventurers. Others have simply stopped selling their own lines of gear, like the Appalachian Mountain Club used to do. But some of the names in gear catalogues and guides from the 1920s and 1930s are still familiar today, such as Duluth Trading or L.L. Bean. Unless they lived near the L.L. Bean store in Freeport, Maine, hikers who wanted to pull together all the gear they needed for their weekend or weeklong hike couldn't go to one store to buy what they needed. Instead, they had to rely on mail order from a wide variety of manufacturers, businesses, hiking clubs and individuals. Just like today, they had to be willing to spend a fair amount of money to fully outfit themselves, and if they wanted the lightest and most comfortable gear and food, the price was even higher.

But it was nevertheless quite possible to purchase what you needed for your hike from various suppliers, and by the 1930s, several of the AT maintaining clubs were publishing lists of suggested gear, complete with commentary on quality, price and details on weight and durability, as well as where to write to get what you wanted. Just like today, "expert" hikers and campers provided advice on what to buy, what to pack and how to camp. That advice appeared in magazines and newspapers, and while the language can sound a bit stilted to our modern ears, the advice wasn't really all that different: buy the lightest and most durable gear you can find, pack the absolute minimum of what you need and through trial and error you'll figure out what works best for you. Of course, "the absolute minimum of what you need" could be a good bit more in the 1930s or the 1940s than it is today, but the advice on what to pack still held true: pack as little as possible. As Arthur Comey of the New England Trail Conference put it in a pamphlet called "Going Light" in 1938:

> *Most of us go into the woods for recreation: to enjoy ourselves, to get away from city life for a bit, to find nature unspoiled by man. We follow the foot trail rather than the highway, and camp out rather than seek lodging and meals provided by others. We cheerfully carry our belongings and our food on our backs to secure greater freedom to roam. But if we take too much, especially if our muscles are soft from city life, our burden may cause us so much suffering as to spoil the trip....Maximum comfort with minimum weight is our goal.*

In fact, despite the heavier gear, with careful planning, a backpacker in the 1920s or 1930s could keep their base weight almost as light as what AT hikers shoot for today. For example, in an April 1927 article in the *St. Louis Post Dispatch*, the outdoor writer Horace Kephart described his kit for a three-night hike in the Smokies. He favored the Duluth canvas packsack (2.5 pounds); the Fiala sleeping bag made with "no-hide fur" (5 pounds); the Hike-lite one-man tent with bobbinet front (2.75 pounds); a waterproof Boy Scout ground cloth (2 pounds); a trail axe (2 pounds); a metal cooking kit consisting of a frying pan, two pots, utensils and a cup (3 pounds); spare underwear and socks (1.5 pounds); an electric torch (flashlight) with spare batteries (1.5 pounds); and various small items like matches, twine and so on (1 pound). This recommended set of gear came in at just under 22 pounds. Kephart seemed to subsist on bread, bacon, cheese, cereal, dried fruit and evaporated milk, so his overall food weight was low compared to many hikers—just 8 pounds for three nights on the trail—making his total weight just a hair under 30 pounds, not counting water. That's a total weight that most backpackers would be reasonably satisfied with today. But Kephart was an exception. The archives of the Appalachian Trail contain many lists of what to pack and which items to purchase, and in those lists, hikers were generally advised to expect to carry at least 30 to 35 pounds of gear and another 1½ to 2 pounds of food per person per day (plus water). All told, a backpacker on the AT in its early decades typically began his or her journey with between 40 to 50 pounds if they were out for a long weekend of hiking.

For example, in the January 1952 issue of the *Appalachian Trailway News*, the quarterly newsletter of the Appalachian Trail Conference, a member described what he and his wife carried on the trail for a full week in Maine the previous year. "Everyone agrees the weight should be kept down, but the average city dweller whose camping is restricted to overnight affairs for 50 weeks of the year, wants to know exactly the items he ought to take for a week." Here is the author's advice:

- *Frame pack with shoulder pads (husband)*
- *Rucksack with shoulder pads (wife)*
- *Two sleeping bags (down)*
- *Cooking and eating utensils*
- *Poncho with hood (husband)*
- *Raincoat and hat (wife)*
- *Clothing and personal articles*
- *First aid kit*
- *Two flashlights with extra bulb*
- *One canteen*
- *A full match case*
- *Two Turkish towels*
- *Toilet paper*
- *Notebook and pencil*
- *Powder for washing*
- *One yard course cotton cloth*

Appalachian Trail hiker with a knapsack, circa 1950. *Potomac Appalachian Trail Club Archives.*

When they added up the weight of all their items, food included, this couple hit the trail with the man carrying fifty-two pounds and the woman with thirty-five pounds. Because they intended to stay only in trail shelters, they forswore a tent, thereby saving at least four pounds, and they intended to use only dead wood for their fires and so left the ubiquitous (in those days) short-handled axe at home, saving a few more pounds. Their food consisted largely of canned, dehydrated and powdered items, but they ate full meals for dinner each night, cooked either over a fire or with a tablet stove. The gendered nature of the weight distribution was typical in the advice literature for AT hikers. In a 1942 essay on hiking the entire AT in the Smokies with his wife, one ATC member described the distribution of their eighty-eight pounds of gear and food as being similar—fifty-eight pounds for him, thirty pounds for her. The not-so-subtle implication of this kind of advice was that without a man to carry the heavier load, a female backpacker couldn't manage a long trip on the trail. Given the era, it's not so surprising to find this kind of thinking, but it's worth noting that broad generalizations about who could and who could not manage to carry the gear and food necessary for a successful hike flew in the face of the lived experienced of many female backpackers of the day, some of whom—like the Three Musketeers in Vermont or Mary Kilpatrick of the Philadelphia Trail Club (the first woman to walk every step of the trail)—all managed just fine on the trail.

One of the truisms about hiking and backpacking is that as these activities have become more popular, suppliers have consistently come out with lighter, more comfortable and generally more durable equipment. The most innovative (meaning the lightest and most durable) equipment has come with a growing price tag, but the larger the market for outdoor gear has become, the more suppliers have entered that market. And the more suppliers there are, the lower the prices of some items have gotten. What follows is a brief history of that gear and how it has evolved over the one hundred years of the trail's existence.

Packs

In 1908, a Norwegian inventor named Ole Bergan created the precursor to the modern backpack. His first "knapsack," a name coined by the American Henry Merriam several decades earlier, had a cloth sack attached to a wooden frame made from juniper that he bent to fit his back. That wooden frame wasn't especially comfortable, so before long, he had replaced it with a tubular steel frame and marketed his knapsack to an international audience of outdoorsmen and women—hunters, climbers and hikers. More than two decades later, Appalachian Trail hikers were being advised to purchase a Bergan knapsack for their hikes. "Frame pack; suitable for heavy loads; prevents chafing, sweating and abrasion," said one set of gear recommendations. The men's size knapsack weighed in at just an ounce over 4 pounds and the smaller women's version at 3 pounds. The 1931 price for the men's version was $16.50, which seems like it must have been reasonably priced. But if you compare the purchasing power of Americans in the early 1930s to what it is now in the early 2020s, that pack cost more than $300, putting it in line with the cost of many ultralight backpacks being recommended to hikers these days. In other words, the Bergan knapsack was a top-of-the-line backpack, one that only more prosperous hikers could afford. Just like today, hikers without that kind of money to spend had plenty of other options. It's impossible to know which backpacks were the most popular in the trail's first decades, but based on what one can see in photographs in the archives, the most popular options used by AT hikers in the 1920s, 1930s and 1940s were the Bergan knapsack, the L.L. Bean pack basket and the Trapper Nelson Pack Board, which came in three sizes, all of them heavier and much less comfortable than the Bergan but much cheaper. The largest of the Trapper Nelson options, weighing in at 5.75 pounds, was only $7.50 in 1931. Because the 1930s were also the decade of the Great Depression, even spending $7.50 on a luxury item like a backpack would have been possible for only a limited number of hikers, but the price of the Trapper Nelson was half that of the Bergan knapsack.

Several years ago, a friend of mine gave me her first husband's old Trapper Nelson pack. "Pack board" doesn't exactly describe what it was like, because instead of being a single board with shoulder straps, it had two very straight wooden uprights, suspended from each other by three steel rods and held off the hiker's back with two canvas bands, one that hit just below the shoulder blades and the other in the vicinity of the hips. There was no hip belt, but there were two padded canvas shoulder straps. When I tried it on, my first reaction was, "This isn't so bad." But then I added weight into the tan canvas sack, and those shoulder straps immediately began to dig into my shoulders. I could feel the steel rods against my spine. I suspect I would have been able to hike with that pack for about thirty minutes, at which point I would have given up and gone home. But the Trapper Nelson was a top-

Knapsack with a birch bark poncho, Vermont, 1930. *Green Mountain Club Archives, Vermont Historical Society.*

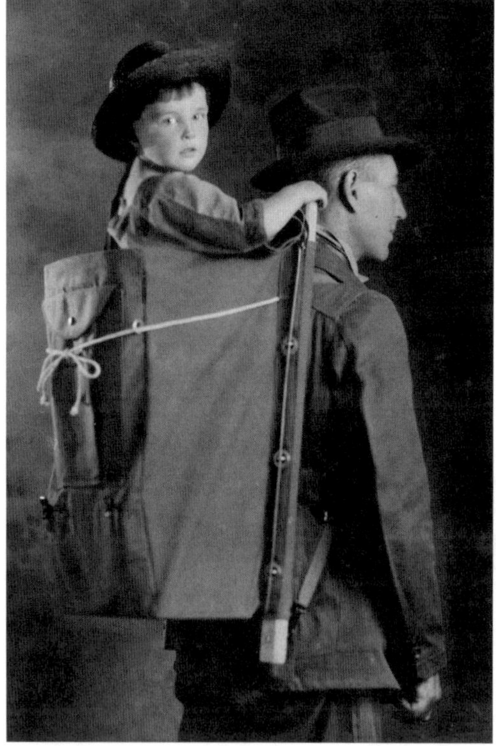

Above: Hikers with knapsacks at Chimney Pond in Baxter State Park, Maine, 1939. *Appalachian Trail Conservancy Archives.*

Left: Lloyd Nelson with his daughter Lois in a Trapper Nelson backpack, circa 1922. *HistoryLink.org, used with permission.*

selling pack by all accounts, and so despite its medieval torture device vibe, plenty of AT hikers used it.

Much more popular in the Northeast, at least in the archival photo collections, was the L.L. Bean pack basket. Those pack baskets looked exactly like their name implies. They were relatively light as the old pack options went—around three and a half pounds—and were made of interwoven ash slats. The structure of the pack was, of course, quite rigid. It came with a waterproof canvas cover and had a capacity of "four pecks." In case you don't remember how much a peck is (or was), four pecks works out to around thirty-five liters. At a cost of only $5.25, the L.L. Bean basket was a much less pricy alternative for the average hiker, and while it couldn't have been all that comfortable to hike with, it was very popular with hikers in the Northeast in the trail's early decades.

In 1952, something wonderful happened in the world of backpacking. That year, a Colorado couple named Dick and Nina Kelty started selling a revolutionary new backpack with an external aluminum frame and a nylon pack. Jack Abert, founder of the Camp Trails company, is credited with inventing the aluminum external frame pack, but it was the Kelty design that quickly took off in a wider market, while Abert's company largely focused on selling to the Scouting market. Much like the old Trapper Nelsons or L.L. Bean pack baskets, the frames of the Camp Trails packs were essentially straight rods of aluminum. The Kelty packs were lighter and more comfortable than the older packs and pack boards but could have been better. The first Kelty frames were made from surplus aircraft aluminum, and the first packs were likewise made from military surplus material—in this case, parachute fabric. The new Kelty packs were contoured to the general shape of the human back, and perhaps most important of all, there was a padded waist belt that redistributed some of the weight of the pack to the hiker's hips and away from the shoulders. According to the company's website, Dick Kelty came up with the idea for the hip belt after putting the ends of the pack's frame into the back pockets of his jeans and noticing how much easier it was to carry the pack. Based on that experience, he asked Nina to sew a hip belt for their new design, and the rest, as they say, is history. Those new Kelty packs were much more comfortable to wear and carry, and the redistribution of weight meant that hikers with less upper-body strength could carry the weight they needed for increasingly long forays into the mountains. To say that the Kelty pack revolutionized the backpacking world would be an understatement because before long several companies had sprung up producing imitations, each of which included new features to make them competitive with the original

Right: Hiker with pack basket on Mount Katahdin, Maine, 1934. *Appalachian Mountain Club Archives.*

Below: Early version of the Kelty backpack, circa 1960. *Kelty Inc.*

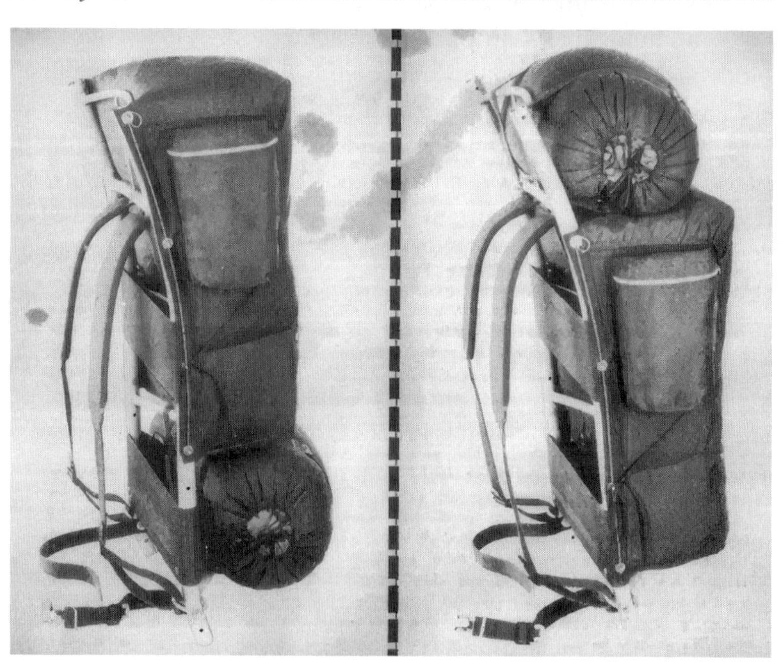

Hikers on the trail with early external frame backpacks, 1971. *Appalachian Trail Conservancy Archives.*

Kelty design. Some of those features included zippered side pockets, two-compartment designs that let hikers store heavy items in the lower reaches of the pack while keeping those items easily accessible through a front opening, better contouring of the frame and, eventually, the shifting of the pack's frame from external to internal.

Credit for the front-loading compartmental design goes to the JanSport corporation, founded in 1967 by a Seattle, Washington couple—Murray Peltz and Jan Lewis (for whom the company is named)—and their friend Skip Yowell. Peltz was an industrial design student, and for an entry into a design competition in 1966, he created an adjustable aluminum frame for a backpack that won the top prize. Peltz asked his girlfriend, Jan Lewis, to design and sew a pack to go with the frame and promised her that if the product took off they would found and name a company after her, hence the name. Like the other companies producing backpacks for serious hikers, JanSport and Kelty also revolutionized the lives of day hikers by producing smaller frameless packs appropriate for a short hike. It's hard now to imagine life in the modern world without those smaller day packs, but they are derived from the earlier knapsack and later backpack designs of the first half of the twentieth century. JanSport's packs hit the market right at the moment that backpacking was taking off as an activity in the United States, and the wider availability of sturdy, lighter and increasingly comfortable packs from companies like Kelty and JanSport helped fuel the growth in backpacking. My first real backpack was a JanSport I bought in the mid-1970s, and it was sturdy enough that I gave it to a young man in my sons' Boy Scout troop in the 2010s for him to use as a first pack. It still had my 1970s AT "Maine to Georgia" patch sewn on the front.

Improvements in backpack design, weight, comfort and durability all contributed to the rising popularity of backpacking by making overnight trips more feasible for more people, but packs were only one of the innovations in outdoor equipment that helped open up the backcountry—and the Appalachian Trail—to tens of thousands of overnight hikers who might never have gone there otherwise. After all, packs were just the means of conveyance for all the rest of the gear, gear that used to weigh quite a lot compared to what's available today.

Tents

From the 1920s until the 1960s, most hikers planning to spend the night on the Appalachian Trail had two very clear options: they could carry a tent or tarp to sleep in or under or they could plan on sleeping in one of the increasing number of trail shelters. Because the number of hikers on the AT remained fairly low until the 1960s, counting on sleeping in a trail shelter was not a bad plan except in a few of the most popular locations, like the Great Smoky Mountains National Park or Shenandoah National Park. But even those sections of the trail saw substantially fewer hikers than they do today, so finding a space on the floor or in a bunk in one of those shelters was, if not a certainty, at least very likely. Most hikers who planned on spending the night in a shelter at least carried a lightweight tarp or large poncho, just in case, but in general they showed a high degree of confidence in being able to sleep under the roof of a shelter. Hikers on the Appalachian Trail have always been (mostly) very willing to accommodate other hikers in the shelters, even if it meant squeezing together more tightly than they might have preferred, so it was only in the most extreme cases that hikers had to make do outdoors, at least until the early 1970s, when the trail started becoming much more popular.

Those hikers who did carry some sort of personal shelter with them before the 1960s likely had either a military-style pup tent or just a tarp of some sort that they could string up between two trees or roll up in if it was raining too hard. Those old pup tents weren't popular because they were light, because they weren't. They were popular because they were small and easy to set up. They were available at most military surplus stores, and by the late 1960s, they even had mosquito netting and a floor. The name "pup tent" is much older than the Appalachian Trail. It turns out that the pup tent first came into general use during the American Civil War, and apparently, soldiers called it that because it wasn't fit for a dog, much less a man. The original design of the pup tent was a center pole setup, a kind of inverted triangle, with a door in the front and two sloping walls in the back. The hiker or hikers slept with their heads near the door and their feet at the bottom of the pyramid. This simple tent structure has made a comeback with ultralight hikers in the past decade. Some of the lightest tents on the market today use the same design but with a trekking pole as the center support. Like the old pup tents, some have floors and some don't. Hikers on the AT used either small (one- or two-person) or large (three- or four-person) versions of these tents on the trail, although the larger ones tended to be used more in the case where some members of the hiking club drove ahead and set up camp for everyone else rather than being carried by a hiker. They were, after all, made of canvas and could be very heavy, especially when wet. Those old canvas tents weren't especially waterproof either. To keep the rain out, hikers had to rub paraffin into their tents regularly and had to dig trenches around their tents to keep the rain from flooding in around their sleeping bags. Of course, digging a trench meant carrying a small shovel. I don't think I've seen a hiker with a shovel on the Appalachian Trail since the late 1970s.

Like so many other areas of backpacking and hiking gear, the Second World War fueled significant innovation in tent design and construction. Canvas fabric was just too heavy, so companies manufacturing tents for the military turned increasingly to lighter-weight cotton with various types of

Above: Trail scout Roy Ozmer with his pup tent on the Appalachian Trail, circa 1930s. *Appalachian Trail Conservancy Archives.*

Left: Eureka Draw-Tite Tent, 1965. *Author's collection.*

waterproofing sprayed or brushed on. But during the later stages of the war, a revolutionary new fabric displaced cotton and canvas in the manufacturing of tents for the military: nylon. Invented by the DuPont Corporation in the mid-1930s, nylon was durable, water-resistant (but not waterproof) and, most importantly, light. The original use for nylon was stockings for women, but after the American entry into the war, DuPont ceased the production of nylon stockings and shifted to the manufacture of parachutes and tents for the military. Following the war, the Eureka Tent & Awning Company in Binghamton, New York, which had also been a major supplier of tents to the military, turned to the manufacture of tents for the camping public. Its "Draw-Tite" tent was the first free-standing, easy-to-set-up nylon tent for the commercial camping market, and it was a hit right away. The design of those original Draw-Tite tents is still so common that you see versions of them in campgrounds all over the world today. Before long, Eureka began selling smaller, easy-to-set-up backpacking tents, and their success encouraged a number of other companies like the Gerry company of Boulder, Colorado, to produce similarly light and easy-to-set-up versions.

Almost completely forgotten now is one innovation in design that just wasn't destined to last: the tube tent. Morgan Somerville, who hiked the entire trail in the 1970s with one of those tube tents, described them this way:

> *It was fairly heavy plastic. I'm just guessing here it was probably 10 mil and the ones I remember were all fluorescent orange. They were tubes of plastic that were about eight feet long and you were supposed to use things like pebbles or maybe a walnut or something like that to tie your rope in three different places on the end. And you had to use a stick to hold one corner up. They were efficient, they were light. But they did not breathe at all, so you always had lots of condensation in them, and if you weren't on a perfectly flat place you tended to slide out over time because they were so slippery. They were sort of like a large heavy duty trash bag without a bottom in it.*

Not surprisingly, tube tents didn't become a staple of the Appalachian Trail hiker gear list. By the late 1970s, canvas tents had all but disappeared from the Appalachian Trail, and hikers were much happier. Their tents weighed so much less, were so much more waterproof and were almost as durable as the heavy, drippy canvas tents of the early days of the trail. They had mosquito netting for their doors and air vents, so life inside the tent was much more enjoyable, especially at night. These days, there are few night sounds in the Appalachian Mountains more enjoyable to listen to than several hundred mosquitos angrily buzzing against the netting of one's tent door, unable to get to your blood. No longer did hikers have to pull their sleeping bag over their heads to keep the biting insects at bay, which means they slept so much better.

Over the decades since the introduction of those first Eureka and Gerry models, tents have gotten better and better, lighter and lighter. And the more they improve, the more accessible the backcountry becomes to the average person. Given how much more crowded the Appalachian Trail has become, hikers can no longer count on being able to find a space in a trail shelter, so having some sort of personal shelter like a tent or a hammock tent is almost a requirement these days. Of course, one could hike with just a shower curtain to roll up in, as Emma Gatewood famously did on her first hike of the AT, or a tarp, as so many hikers did until tents got much lighter. But not many hikers today are willing to opt for that minimalist approach.

At some point in the relatively recent past, meaning two or three decades ago, hammock camping became popular with a small but dedicated group of AT hikers. Hammocks, of course, have been part of human history for a very long time—perhaps thousands of years—but as shelter options carried by backpackers, they were largely limited to a tiny fringe of hikers. But like almost every innovation in backpacking gear since 1940, it was World War II that led to the modern trend in hammock camping, albeit many decades after the war. In 1942, the U.S. Army began using what it called the "jungle hammock" in the Pacific theater of operations, and those jungle hammocks are the progenitors of today's hammock tents. Here's what the U.S. Army quartermaster had to say about them in late 1942:

> *During the wet season, when rain fell incessantly for hours, flooding bivouac areas and preventing tents from being pitched, jungle hammocks kept the troops "high and dry during the sleeping hours." Some men in rear areas consistently preferred them for the better protection they gave against crawling and flying insects and slept in them as often as they could.*

In the 1950s, a young man from North Carolina named Tom Hennessy bought one of those jungle hammocks in an army surplus store and was captivated. He used that old hammock tent until he made the mistake of loaning it to a friend who never returned it. Like any good entrepreneur, Hennessy then just made his own. Over the years, he kept modifying the army's original design until, in 1998, he decided he should start selling his hammock tents to the general public. The first Hennessy hammock tents went to market the following year. Today, of course, there are many imitators to compete with that first mass-market hammock tent, but the basic design Hennessy came up with at home hasn't changed all that much from hammock to hammock. Hikers devoted to their hammock tents love the fact that they do not require a patch of level ground—just two trees sturdy enough to support the hiker's weight and spaced widely enough to stretch the hammock out fully. As with almost any aspect of backpacking these days, there are debates about the ecological impact of hammock tents versus regular tents, with passionate supporters on both sides. Hung properly with straps instead of rope, hammock tents make it possible for hikers to sleep without compressing the ground beneath them. But if the hammock isn't hung correctly, it can cause lasting damage to the trees it is suspended from.

Sleeping Bags

The modern sleeping bag, in its simplest form just a large blanket with either a zipper or snaps to enclose the sleeper, has been around since the end of the nineteenth century. There are competing claims for who "invented" the modern version of the sleeping bag, but it seems most likely that it was the Norwegian explorer Fridtjof Nansen who designed something closer to what we use today. Nansen had spent a good bit of time with Inuit people during his explorations of the Arctic, and he saw how warmly they slept under seal skins. In the late 1880s, Nansen had some of those seal skins sewn together into bags that would hold three people, which he used during a ski crossing of Greenland. The following year, a Norwegian company began producing similar items, but for individual sleepers, and the modern sleeping bag became a commercial product.

By the time hikers began spending the night on the Appalachian Trail in the 1920s and 1930s, they had many sleeping bag options to choose from, and the makers of some of those bags served up some pretty big claims. "Your dreams come true when you sleep on air in a luxurious, water and windproof Comfort Sleeping Pocket. You are assured the most comfortable and satisfactory arrangement for out-of-door sleeping." This enticing 1924 ad for the Comfort Sleeping Pocket from the Metropolitan Camp Goods Company of Athol, Massachusetts, said that the Sleeping Pocket was perfect for camping, canoeing, yachting, motor boating or "vocational purposes" and that the pocket was recommended for "Stockmen, Forest Service, Prospectors, Sportsmen, Exploration Parties, Convalescents, and all who sleep for it complies with all requirements." Who wouldn't want a sleeping system that complies with all requirements? Of course, given that the Sleeping Pocket weighed more than six pounds, it was unlikely to be popular with hikers.

While it was possible to purchase a bag that weighed less than six pounds, modern temperature ratings for bags weren't part of the product descriptions in those days, so it is likely that the lighter bags were what today we would think of as "summer weight" bags. A 1931 list of recommended gear from the PATC includes options from the Appalachian Mountain Club, Fiala Outfits and the previously mentioned Metropolitan Camp Goods Company. The AMC bag was the lightest and least expensive option, but it was little more than two blankets sewn together, requiring the hiker to also carry an outer cover both for extra warmth and waterproofing. In his "Packing Light" essay, Arthur Comey, one of the founders of the ATC, described those old AMC bags this way: "Sufficient for the average person from May to October, provided on cool nights he secures plenty of browse and wears all his apparel." The top end of the bag could be buttoned together on cool nights, and the lower blanket was five inches longer, allowing the hiker to encase the chin and neck in the blanket as well. But on very cool nights, hikers were advised, "all one's woolen clothing may need to be worn." Comey also had some thoughts about what should *not* be worn while sleeping. "Care should be taken to remove belt, garters, tie, shoes, or other bindings that might hamper circulation." It's hard to imagine someone wearing their shoes inside their sleeping bag, but Comey must have seen someone do that, hence his advice to take those shoes (and ties and garters) off.

For hikers who didn't want to spring for a sleeping bag but did want to stay warm at night, the early advice literature recommended army or navy blankets as a viable option, but hikers were warned to be sure to also bring a waterproof tarp or poncho to prevent their blankets (or sleeping bags) from getting soaked. In 1921, an army blanket could be purchased from Abercrombie & Fitch that weighed in at five or three pounds (khaki color only) for about half the price of a good sleeping bag. And if you were winter camping in higher elevations or in New England stretches of the trail, you could always go with the "luxurious eiderdown robe bed" from Metropolitan Camp Goods. The 1924 advertisements for this warm and toasty sleeping system gave no hint of the weight, but they show a camper in his robe bed lying on the bare snow with a big smile on his face.

Fortunately for the average Appalachian Trail hiker, sleeping bag technology improved as rapidly as improvements in packs and tents, if not more so. By the 1950s, again as a result of innovations during the war, sleeping bag weights had dropped, and their protection against the cold had improved. The mummy-style bag had gone into mass production at several companies, and down had become the go-to filling for the serious hiker. Some gear aficionados argue that Roy and Alice Holubar of Boulder, Colorado, were the first to make and sell sleeping bags that we would recognize today—a nylon shell, synthetic or down filling and a zipper on the side or top for easy access. Whether or not the Holubars were the inventors of the modern recreational sleeping bag, as early as 1954 they were offering such bags for sale in their mail-order catalogues. By the 1960s, it was difficult to find a sleeping bag that buttoned or laced up because full-length zippers had become ubiquitous features of the modern sleeping bag, and hikers have been the better for it ever since. It's worth remembering, though, that for the first four decades of the trail's existence, bags that zipped up the side were a homemade novelty, not a standard item in anyone's pack. Today's AT hiker is faced with simply too many choices of sleeping bag, and at the risk of saying that sometimes history *does* repeat itself, sleeping quilts have returned to the Appalachian Trail as increasingly popular items. They don't weigh nearly as much as those old army blankets, but the principle is the same.

Today's hikers often look back at the hikers of yore and think that they were much tougher than we are today. It is true that they carried more weight, their gear was uncomfortable and they had to be able to build cooking fires in all kinds of weather. But when it came to sleeping, the hikers of yesteryear wanted to be comfortable too. While many of the early AT hikers may have slept on the cold, hard ground, they didn't have to. Sleeping pad technology was far older than the Appalachian Trail—far, far older—and hasn't changed very much since its invention in the nineteenth century. The first company to begin marketing "air beds"—what we would call air mattresses today—was the Massachusetts-based Pneumatic Mattress & Cushion Company, which began producing air beds in 1889. There is even some evidence of early blow-up beds in use, although not in commercial distribution, as early as the 1850s. Within a decade of the Pneumatic Mattress company's rollout of air beds, a number of companies were offering competing products. For example, the Mechanical Manufacturing Company marketed its "Perfection" air mattress that offered "10,000 Nights of Luxury" to the happy sleeper. By the time hikers began venturing onto the Appalachian Trail, it was possible to buy versions of those air mattresses purpose-built for camping. Looking at ads for those hundred-year-old sleeping pads, they hardly look different from the ones we sleep on today. But their makers promised things like, "Only the very finest materials enter into the construction of this mattress—strictly handmade throughout....Coated with the best quality of live rubber. Stays are of strong heavy tape and they will not break." Although available already in the 1920s, inflatable sleeping pads must not have been very popular with AT hikers because they almost never show up in recommended lists of hiking gear. Perhaps an air bed just felt like too much luxury.

Shoes

Without the proper footwear, no one's hike turns out well, whether it is for a few hours, a few days, a few weeks or months. That was true in 1925 when the Appalachian Trail began, and it is still true today. Of course, what hikers wear on the trail to keep their feet happy has changed dramatically over the past one hundred years. For example, when was the last time someone asked you what kind of hobnails you put in the soles of your boots or shoes? In 1925, choosing the right hobnail for your boot could make the difference between an enjoyable hike and one where you found yourself slipping and sliding over every rock. It's almost certain that hikers in the 1920s would feel very envious of the boots and shoes we wear on the trail today. But it is also fair to say that the boots worn on the Appalachian Trail until after World War II were much more stylish than ours. In archival photographs, it is very common to see hikers wearing supple leather boots that laced up to just below the knee joint. They were practical, but they also just looked good. They came in variable heights, from six to nine to fifteen inches high, and the tallest ones—at least based on what one sees in those old photos—were the most popular. They were likely hot to wear in the summer and fall, but they looked awfully comfortable and had the added benefit of protecting you—at least as high as the top of your shins—from poison ivy, briars, nettles and even snakebites.

These days, of course, hikers love to wear light hiking shoes, trail runners and even sandals when hiking on the Appalachian Trail, although plenty still wear more traditional boots or at least hard-soled shoes. How did we get from those fifteen-inch-high boots to today's lightweight footwear? The story begins in Maine. One of the most popular boots used by backpackers in the Northeast, at least through the end of the Second World War, was the Maine hunting shoe, sold by L.L. Bean. By his own admission, Mr. Bean was not a very successful businessman and loved spending time in the Maine woods hunting and fishing. What he did *not* love was getting blisters or wet feet. To make his own life better, Bean asked a cobbler he knew to make him a pair of boots with rubber bottoms and leather uppers. What he was after was a hunting and fishing boot that was waterproof, combined the fit and comfort of his favorite dress shoes, was light enough to wear all day and was strong enough to deal with the weather in Maine. The boots his friend made for him were good enough that he started taking orders for them and, before long, had sold ninety pairs. Unfortunately, the rubber bottoms on those first boots were not very durable. Bean found a better rubber supplier (Goodyear

Tire), made new pairs for his ninety dissatisfied customers and replaced the ones no one liked. That was in 1912. The rubber soles on the Bean boot, with their chain-style tread, provided much better traction on slippery surfaces, and they were much more durable than the leather soles that were the standard for boots up to that point. That design was so successful that you can still buy versions of those old boots today.

Although the Maine hunting shoe was popular in the soggier and snowier climes of New England, other boots from other companies competed for the hiker and backpacker trade in those early decades of the Appalachian Trail. Among those vying for the attention of backpackers and hikers was the Red Wing Shoe Company, which was marketing its own line of rubber-soled boots, and like L.L. Bean, Red Wing sold boots in a variety of heights, from ankle to lower calf to mid-calf. The boots available from Bean and Red Wing lasted longer and cost less than others on the market, and their hard rubber soles meant that hikers' feet didn't get as easily bruised, making the prospect of a long day on the trail much more inviting for the average hiker.

One of the most ubiquitous logo images seen in parks and on trails these days is the boot sole, usually paired with some sort of "Leave No Trace" message. That sole, the classic design created by the Italian mountaineer Vitale Bramani in 1937, is known as the Vibram sole, a mash-up of Bramani's name. He created the iconic boot sole following the deaths of six of his friends in a climbing accident, which he blamed, in part, on the leather-soled boots they were wearing. To ensure that climbers had better, safer footwear, Bramani designed a rubber sole with the tank track design we know so well. In fact, the first version of the Vibram sole was called the *Carramato*, which means "tank tread" in Italian. The new Vibram soles eliminated the need for

Vibram sole, circa 1970. *Internet Archive.*

hobnails, which I'm sure almost every hiker cheered, because the new soles had such better traction and required no hammering.

Once leather soles and hobnails were a thing of the past, shoemakers began to experiment with other synthetic materials for the rest of the boot. Leather has many advantages, but one of the main disadvantages is that it can be very stiff, making it hard to break in. Surely the most famous of all Appalachian Trail hikers is Emma "Grandma" Gatewood, who was no fan of leather shoes and famously hiked in Converse sneakers. In the last interview she gave before she died in 1973, Gatewood said:

> *After somebody from a store gave me a pair of leather shoes, I walked the Baker Trail in Pennsylvania for 247 miles. They hurt my heel and I had to split them down the back, and then I kind of sewed them back together and that did it. That's the only time I ever had any sores, when I had on leather shoes.*

The other problem with leather, of course, is that once it has soaked up water, it takes a long time to dry.

Emma "Grandma" Gatewood near the end of her first thru hike of the Appalachian Trail, Maine, 1955. *Appalachian Trail Conservancy Archives.*

During the Second World War, shoemakers began to experiment with a variety of synthetic materials that would be lighter, cheaper, at least as durable, quicker to dry and in the end more comfortable to wear. All that experimentation with footwear continued throughout the 1950s and the 1960s. Companies like Red Wing and L.L. Bean came out with several different designs, but the big breakthrough came in the 1970s when Bill and Vieve Gore, along with their son Bob, founded a company to make what they called Gore-Tex. Boot makers began including Gore-Tex—a basement lab creation by the Gore family—in their products, and hikers have had drier feet ever since.

Of course, not everyone wears boots on the trail. Day hikers wear just about anything, and these days it is very common to see backpackers wearing some sort of trail running shoe instead of boots. The history of the trail runner goes back to 1978, when an American mountaineering expedition summited K2 without relying on oxygen. Two members of that team, John Roskelley and Rick Ridgeway, wore Nike LDV running shoes on their one-hundred-mile hike up to the K2 base camp and then back down from there after their successful ascent. They were so enthusiastic about how well those running shoes held up and how comfortable they were to wear that Nike began work on trail running shoes that could double as hiking shoes. The resulting shoe, the Escape, was six years in the making, and this new shoe helped fuel the sport of trail running. It and its many successors from Nike and other brands have now become common footwear for hikers and backpackers on the Appalachian Trail.

Clothing

The clothing hikers wore on the Appalachian Trail has changed just as much over the decades as the packs they carry, the tents they sleep in and the shoes they wear on their feet. If you watch movies from the 1930s in the trail club archives, it's hard not to laugh at some of the attire from those days—jodhpurs with knee-high boots, men wearing vests, ties and sometimes homburg hats. A hiker aesthetic didn't really develop until after the 1960s or 1970s, at least based on those old photos in the archives, but the advice literature for hikers tended to emphasize wool clothing as much as possible for its warmth, durability and moisture-wicking properties. Cotton shirts were also commonly suggested for warmer weather, and until fairly

Hiker on the trail circa 1970. *Appalachian Trail Conservancy Archives.*

recently, hikers were advised to wear denim or twill pants for their durability. By the 1960s, that style had changed rather radically because your average hiker was not going to be caught dead wearing the almost formal clothing recommended for hikers in earlier decades. What one sees in the photos from the 1960s and the 1970s is a rainbow of colored T-shirts, including lots of tie-dye, cut-off denim shorts or gym shorts over striped athletic socks, big clunky boots, cotton work shirts and tank tops. It's not until the early 1990s that nylon clothing really starts to show up in the photographs as the more common choice.

These days, it's common to see hikers on the Appalachian Trail dressed in just about any sort of clothing and carrying just about any kind of gear one can imagine. The choices hikers make about what to carry and what to wear are governed by the weather, how long they intend to hike, whether they'll be camping out or not and how much they are willing to spend on their gear. Looking back over the past one hundred years of AT history, one could say the same thing about the hikers of the 1930s or the 1950s. The biggest difference is that today's hikers have so many more choices and so much better access to those choices through stores catering specifically to hikers and the many shopping opportunities on the Internet. Their gear is lighter, and their clothing is more comfortable. They can go out on the trail wearing whatever they grab out of the closet or dresser, or they can spend hundreds or even thousands of dollars on the lightest, most up-to-date gear. But whatever they wear and whatever they carry, the Appalachian Trail is still a long brown path up and down mountain slopes, marked out by white rectangular blazes for them to follow, just as it was in the 1930s.

TRAIL SHELTERS

FOUNDATIONS OF AN EPHEMERAL COMMUNITY

Shelter Camps: These are the usual accompaniments of the trails which have been built in the White and Green Mountains. They are the trail's equipment for use. They should be located at convenient distances so as to allow a comfortable day's walk between each. They should be equipped always for sleeping and certain of them for serving meals—after the fashion of the Swiss chalets. Strict regulation is essential to provide that equipment is used and not abused.

—Benton MacKaye, 1921

It is too elementary to require elaboration, that the Appalachian Trail system requires a series of accommodations along its route. In the ideal, this should be a dual system. Shelters for those who wish to camp. Wherever possible, listed available public accommodations for those who prefer to expend their energy other than in carrying gear.... The time has come to survey the route and make a construction program.

—Myron Avery's annual report to the Appalachian Trail Conference Board of Managers, 1937

When ATC Chairman Myron Avery declared the Appalachian Trail complete at the 1937 meeting of the Appalachian Trail Conference in Gatlinburg, Tennessee, he knew that if the various constituent trail clubs were going to maintain the enthusiasm of their volunteers, those volunteers would need a new task. With the trail completed from Maine to Georgia, they needed something to do, something to expend their trail volunteer energy on. The idea of building a chain of shelters along the trail was as old as the proposal for the trail itself, although Benton MacKaye certainly had something a bit more elaborate and a bit less rustic in mind. He was, after all, not much of a camper by the time he proposed the AT in 1921, so the thought of a Swiss-style chalet serving a hot meal to hungry hikers probably sounded a lot better than an Adirondack-style lean-to, open to the elements on one side and with no meal service anywhere in sight. But both MacKaye and Avery understood that if the Appalachian Trail was really going to catch on with hikers, those hikers would need somewhere to sleep if they didn't want to stay in a tent, or they would want a place to have a picnic with family and friends. Avery also insisted that those new shelters should be close to a consistent water source, if possible, should be sited in such a way that they had pleasing views and should have a privy for hikers who preferred to not do their business behind a tree. Avery also understood that it was going to take a lot of effort to make the AT into a popular recreation destination and that having shelters in pleasing spots with easy access to water and a privy would go a long way toward making the trail more accessible and attractive to more people.

As mentioned earlier, it was at that Gatlinburg meeting that Myron Avery and Ed Ballard from the National Park Service quashed any thought that the shelters might be reserved for trail club members. The trail shelters were to open the trail to *all* hikers. Avery knew something already about these matters from his other trail-related role as president of the Potomac Appalachian Trail Club (PATC). Under Avery's leadership, the PATC had already built its first lean-to (the Lewis Spring lean-to, removed long ago) and three cabins along the trail, confusingly called "shelters" in those days. The club already was acting as a concessionaire in Shenandoah National Park, and club members had decided that their cabins (shelters) would be for club members but that the lean-tos they built (or were planning to build) along the trail would be for all hikers to enjoy. Avery was also familiar with the trail shelters the Green Mountain Club had already built along the Long Trail, the shelters and cabins belonging to the Dartmouth Outing Club and the extensive chain of high mountain huts maintained by the Appalachian Mountain Club. The newly completed Appalachian Trail shared more than two hundred miles of trail with these three organizations, each of which had varying rules about whether hikers needed to pay to use their facilities. He wanted the rest of the shelters along the AT to be open to all at no cost. The egalitarian principles laid down by Avery and Ballard at that 1937 meeting ensured that the Appalachian Trail was going to be a people's trail.

Hikers on Mary's Rock in Shenandoah National Park, 1930. *Potomac Appalachian Trail Club Archives.*

Two hikers taking a break at a shelter in Massachusetts, 1951. *Appalachian Trail Conservancy Archives.*

Hikers on the Appalachian Trail on Pico Mountain, Vermont, 1958. *Appalachian Trail Conservancy Archives.*

Setting up camp on the trail in Maryland, 1950. *Potomac Appalachian Trail Club Archives.*

Above: Hikers on a summit in the Great Smoky Mountains National Park, 1960. *Potomac Appalachian Trail Club Archives*.

Left: Ready to start the hike, circa 1970s. *Appalachian Trail Conservancy Archives*.

Left: Plank walkway through a wetland on the Appalachian Trail in Maine, circa 1970s. *Appalachian Trail Conservancy Archives*.

Below: An inquisitive jay in the White Mountains of New Hampshire, circa 1980s. *Appalachian Trail Conservancy Archives*.

The Delaware Water Gap from the Appalachian Trail in Pennsylvania, circa 1980s.
Appalachian Trail Conservancy Archives.

Fall colors on one of the many beautiful ponds along the trail in Maine, circa 1980s.
Appalachian Trail Conservancy Archives.

Day hikers at an overlook in Virginia, circa 1980s. *Potomac Appalachian Trail Club Archives.*

Hiking upward through the fog on the trail in Connecticut, circa 1980s. *Appalachian Trail Conservancy Archives.*

On Franconia Ridge in New Hampshire, circa 1980s. *Appalachian Trail Conservancy Archives.*

Along the trail in Southern Virginia, 1984. *Appalachian Trail Conservancy Archives.*

Above: In the White Mountains of New Hampshire, circa 1980s. *Appalachian Trail Conservancy Archives*.

Left: Hiking through the snow in North Carolina, circa 1985. *Appalachian Trail Conservancy Archives*.

Above: Modern nylon dome tents on the trail in New Jersey, circa 1990s. *Appalachian Trail Conservancy Archives*.

Right: Toward the summit in Vermont, 1988. *Appalachian Trail Conservancy Archives*.

Top: Hikers on the trail in New York, circa 1990. *Appalachian Trail Conservancy Archives.*

Bottom: Sunset on Blackrock Mountain, Shenandoah National Park, 2016. *Photograph by author.*

Top: Clouds over the trail in Virginia, 2012. *Potomac Appalachian Trail Club Archives*.

Bottom: The Green Tunnel on Blue Mountain in Virginia, 2017. *Photograph by author.*

Hazel Mountain Overlook, Shenandoah National Park, 2016. *Photograph by author.*

Waterfall on the trail in North Carolina, 2019. *Photograph by author.*

Morning on Max Patch Mountain, North Carolina, 2021. *Photograph by author.*

Camping at Overmountain Shelter, North Carolina, 2022. *Photograph by Sarah Jones Decker, used with permission.*

The Rainbow Springs Shelter in Maine, 2021. *Photograph by Sarah Jones Decker, used with permission.*

The Overmountain Shelter (torn down in 2023) in Tennessee, 2020. *Photograph by Sarah Jones Decker, used with permission.*

Above: Sunset along the trail in Shenandoah National Park, 2019. *Photograph by author.*

Right: Thru hiker Sarah ("Serendipity") Robison at the conclusion of her traverse of the entire trail in 2021. *Courtesy of Sarah Robison.*

Above: A hiker resting in the Churchill Scott Shelter, Vermont, 2020. *Photograph by Sarah Jones Decker, used with permission.*

Left: The monument on Centerpoint Knob, Pennsylvania, the original halfway point of the Appalachian Trail. *Photograph by author.*

Hikers at the Ashby Gap Shelter, Virginia, circa 1940. *Appalachian Trail Conservancy Archives.*

To help the trail clubs along with their shelter-building efforts, the ATC published plans for lean-tos and their associated privies that included a list of the needed building materials and advice on how to go about building the structures. Although the trail clubs signed onto the shelter building project with varying degrees of enthusiasm, within twenty years it was possible for a hiker on most sections of the trail to find a backwoods structure to sleep in. The vast majority of those early structures were built in the style of the Adirondack lean-to or were in the now-familiar U.S. Forest Service standard post-and-beam style. But even in those early decades of the trail, there was already a reasonably high degree of architectural variability between the different shelters. The fact that they don't all look the same is part of their appeal.

Although Avery saw the shelters as a way to motivate club volunteers and to make the trail more inviting to more hikers, they quickly became much more than just places to stop for a few hours or the night. Architectural historian Jason Miller told me in an interview:

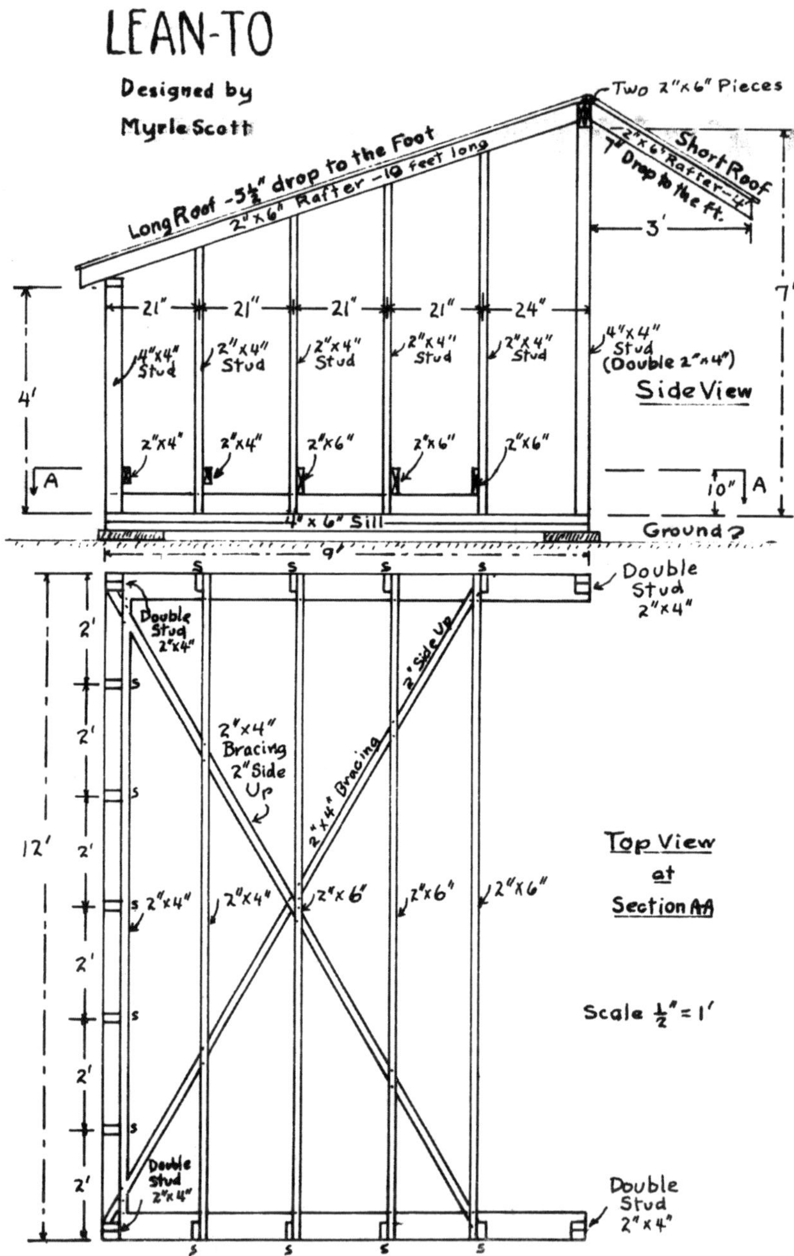

Original plans for lean-to shelters for the Appalachian Trail, circa 1938. *Appalachian Trail Conservancy Archives.*

> *The shelters contribute to Benton MacKaye's idea of a larger community of hikers. They are the physical artifacts of an ephemeral community that changes year by year. Every year, there are continuing hikers and people who do section hikes, there are the day hikers, there are people who touch the trail once and maybe never again, and there are people who touch it for decades. And they all connect at the shelters.*

Because the shelters were (mostly) remote and (mostly) open to the elements, they also gave hikers a much greater sense of being in nature. As Miller sees it, "At the shelters we get to interweave a little bit of our built heritage and our myth history about how we interface with the wilderness and that's kind of what primitive huts do." Hikers stopping at shelters could become quite lyrical about the experience. As one hiker wrote in a shelter register:

> *The light shot through a leafy screen sprinkled with water drops. Wild birds presented their hypnotic symphony. Rocks aren't obstacles, instead they are natural statues of past motion and force. These sights of wilderness I have seen, which others have seen as monsters and remarks on nature's weakness. Take heart, a man is part of wildness and observer at the same time.*
>
> —*New Hampshire, 1973*

Once the chain of shelters was complete, hikers could typically count on finding a wooden structure on or near the trail every ten to fifteen miles along their route. The shelters closest to roads or cities saw and continue to see the most use, while those in more remote locations are most often visited by long-distance hikers journeying north or south. But all the shelters, regardless of location, quickly became the sort of nodes of ephemeral community described by Miller.

After the Appalachian Trail became a national park in 1968, the park service and the forest service pressed the trail clubs to standardize the design of the shelters. Standardization is, after all, an essential value of government agencies seeking efficiency in their operations. Fortunately for hikers, the clubs that maintain the shelters have (largely) successfully resisted the drive toward standardization, and hikers still find a wide variation in design, although the Adirondack lean-to and post-and-beam structures are the most common. In the colder locations of New England, a significant number of the shelters have four walls instead of three, providing hikers with greater shelter from the winter elements. A few of the shelters are buildings that sat along the trail before its creation and have been repurposed for hiker use. One of the most iconic of those, the Overmountain Shelter, was an old red barn that was only recently torn down because it was no longer safe for hikers to use. Unlike today, many of those early lean-to shelters sat on the ground, with dirt floors, and almost all had some sort of fire pit out in front of the opening so that on chilly nights, hikers could build up a fire that would cast warmth into the structure, at least as long as someone kept the fire burning.

A significant number of the early trail shelters in or near the two national parks and in Maine were built by work crews from the Civilian Conservation Corps during the 1930s. Given the CCC's penchant for stone and concrete construction, it should come as no surprise that the all-stone Blood Mountain Shelter in Georgia is one of the surviving CCC structures. Likewise, many of the older shelters in Shenandoah National Park (confusingly called "huts") were built by CCC crews. Those huts have distinctive stone walls with log-and-beam roofs. But CCC crews also built traditional wooden lean-to shelters, including several in Virginia and many in Maine. They just preferred stone and cement.

One of the distinctive features of the Appalachian Trail shelters is the registers that trail clubs place there for hikers to write in. Those old registers took many forms, from school notebooks to accounting ledgers to pocket-sized notepads. They got wet, hikers spilled food or drink on them and they often included illustrations drawn by hikers young and old. Holding them

The Blood Mountain Shelter, Georgia, 2018. *Photograph by the author.*

in your hand today, you are instantly transported back to the 1980s, the 1950s or even the 1930s, when hikers sat at a picnic table or huddled next to a candle or flashlight to scrawl out their messages for others who followed them up and down the trail. In the small number of shelter registers from the 1930s that survive in archives, one can see how these simple structures quickly attracted diverse groups of hikers—church groups, Scouting troops, families, small clusters of friends—as well as individual hikers out for the day, a few days or even a few weeks. By far, though, the largest number of hikers coming to the trail shelters in those early decades of the trail were members of the many trail clubs who had scouted and created the trail and had more recently built the shelters. The archives of the trail clubs also hold newsletters and other promotional materials letting members know when and where hikes would be in a given month, and those hikes often stopped at a trail shelter at midday or toward the end of a hike so that club members could sit, eat, refill their water bottles and sometimes cook a meal.

> *At Velvet Rocks with Russ (of course) and 6 month old Ilana—on her 3rd uphill trek. She babbled happily all the way. May she continue to babble happily uphill on all her hikes!*
>
> —*New Hampshire, 1991*

Hikers who did spend the night at a trail shelter shared news of their hikes, food, firewood and fellowship. They played cards together and sang camping and hiking songs, and much more often than you might expect, they square danced, either to a tune someone played on a fiddle brought along for that purpose or, if the shelter was close to a road (as many were), a hand-cranked record player. More often than not, square dancing at trail shelters was not a spontaneous activity. Instead, dancing was pre-planned by local trail clubs, which published a list of the songs they would be dancing to on a particular hike in their club newsletter. It must have been something for a hiker to see when he or she came around a bend in the trail and found a group of fellow hikers swinging their partners to the words of the caller.

Although square dancing seems to have completely disappeared from the Appalachian Trail community—at least on the trail—all the other things that hikers shared with one another continue to be part of the culture of the community that has grown up around the shelters. Because the shelters were placed at what amounted to a reasonable day's hike from one another, hikers often aimed at the next shelter, or possibly the one after that, for their next place to stop. Unlike today's trail shelters, where hikers most often sleep

Square dancing at the end of a day's hike on the Appalachian Trail, circa 1940. *Appalachian Trail Conservancy Archives.*

on the floor of the structure, the early trail shelters were often fitted out with iron cots with heavy canvas stretched across the springs to provide a comfortable night's sleep—or at least more comfortable than sleeping on the dirt or plank floor of the shelter. But in Maine, many of the original shelters were less comfortable. As longtime trail maintainer and ATC leader Dave Field told me in an interview:

> *All the CCC lean-tos may not have had boards for floors. They used small peeled poles and it took 40 or 50 very tiny little spruce and fir poles to build up a floor. And of course they were awful to sleep on. People don't understand that the first thing you did in those years when you got to a lean-to was cut a bunch of fir bows and wove them into those poles to build up a beautiful springy, fragrant mattress. The next time you got there, you tore out the old ones and put in new ones, which of course would have denuded the forest for miles around if the practice had continued.*

Because there were so few hikers on the trail in the early decades, cutting tree branches to sleep on was feasible. Given how many hikers there are

Hikers at the East Carry Pond Shelter, Maine, 1954. *Appalachian Mountain Club Archives.*

today, as Dave said, that kind of tree trimming would all but kill off the nearby forest.

As hiking became more and more popular, the shelters also saw increasing amounts of use and, sadly, abuse. By the late 1960s, shelter maintainers, who were all trail club volunteers, were submitting more and more reports about problems at the shelters. These included weekend parties that often resulted in large piles of trash; growing amounts of graffiti; the carving of initials and other things into shelter walls, floors and picnic tables; hikers jumping onto the roofs of shelters and punching holes through the fragile shingles; and just generally rowdy behavior by hikers. At the shelters close to roads, non-hikers sometimes saw the shelters as their personal party venues. As the problems grew, the complaints from volunteer maintainers in the trail clubs increased until, in the second half of 1973, the ATC felt it necessary to survey its members and trail club leaders about the future of the trail shelters. Should the shelter system continue as it was despite the problems? Should the shelters be removed from the trail altogether and replaced with tent platforms and/or designated campsites? Or was there some compromise solution? Members and club leaders were invited to chime in, and many of their responses made it painfully clear that there was a significant problem with the shelter system as it currently existed:

> *Vandalism is a growing, unchecked problem and one of the main reasons why our shelters have a dubious future. I have seen many shelters that have more bullet holes in them than the Alamo. What is frightening is that a shelter could be the difference between life and death to a hiker or hikers caught in an unpredictable situation.*
>
> —*New York*

> *The shelter system on the A.T. (except in national forests) is obsolete. The shelters I am acquainted with in Pennsylvania are in such sad shape that most of them should have been removed long ago. There was a time when these shelters served a purpose, but times and attitudes have changed. With the advent of lightweight shelters, stoves and other equipment, the serious A.T. hiker can manage very well without the need for these shelters.*
>
> *—Pennsylvania*

> *Removal of those shelters subjected to constant abuse and vandalism is the most direct and efficient method of dealing with this problem. It angers me to realize that people have invested their own time, money, and talents into building shelters only to have them destroyed by callously indifferent vandals.*
>
> *—Maryland*

> *Recently four friends and I hiked in the Cherokee section of the Appalachian Trail from Tenn. 67 to the Nolichucky River. Three of the five shelters which we visited were inhabitable for a night (Laurel Fork, Cherry Gap and Curley Maple Gap). The other two: Moreland Gap and Grassy Ridge were unbelievable. We collected everything from one gallon Coleman's fluid cans to ex-wire bunks for over an hour. We slept on the roof because the wire bunks were ripped out. It is senseless to build more shelters when those now in use are dumps.*
>
> *—North Carolina*

Not everyone was as sad or angry as these respondents, but the general consensus of those who answered the ATC survey was that *something* had to be done and soon. The eventual solution that the ATC and the trail-maintaining clubs came up with was a hybrid, drawn from the suggestions of hundreds of interested parties. Most of the "problem" shelters were those that were within an easy walk of a road crossing, and over the next few years, most of those shelters were removed altogether or simply relocated to more inaccessible (from the road) locations. New shelters were built in equally difficult-to-reach locations, while still being reasonably spaced from the shelters to the north and the south. Some of the clubs recruited members to act as shelter supervisors, staying at or near their shelters on the weekends during peak hiking season. And the ATC began to invest in what it called the "On the Trail Education System"—a precursor in many ways to the national Leave No Trace campaign—that used volunteers and paid staff

Trash at the Wiggins Spring Shelter, Virginia, 1970. *Appalachian Trail Conservancy Archives.*

to meet with hikers on the trail and educate them about wilderness ethics (and at the same time keep an eye out for problems at certain shelters). The Ridge Runner system in use today derives in part from this earlier approach to meeting hikers on the trail, helping them be better hikers and better stewards of the wilderness.

The one place where things really got out of hand was in Shenandoah National Park, one of the most popular sections of the entire Appalachian Trail. By early 1974, the park's superintendent had had enough of the partying at trail shelters inside the park and declared them off-limits except in a life-threatening situation. Park staff removed all bunks from the shelters inside the park boundaries and posted signs in the shelters informing hikers that anyone found sleeping in the shelters except in the case of an emergency would be subject to a substantial fine. Further, new camping regulations came into force that stipulated that anyone camping within the park and not at a designated campsite had to be completely out of sight from the Appalachian Trail. I was one of the hundreds of AT hikers who ran afoul of this latter change. A friend and I were backpacking in the park during our senior year of high school and had found a level spot that we *thought* was out of sight of the trail. We were about halfway through eating our dinner when two rangers barged into our campsite and informed us, in not very polite terms, that they could see us from the trail and that we had to move. My friend asked if we could finish our dinner, and one of the rangers snarled, "No." Not wanting to pay a fine, we moved.

The Potomac Appalachian Trail Club, which had been maintaining shelters along the Appalachian Trail in the park since before the park even opened, fought a five-year struggle with the federal authorities to get the shelters reopened. Finally, in the late spring of 1979, the park superintendent relented and allowed a limited number of the trail shelters to come back into use, but only a few and only with PATC shelter monitors in place every weekend. Hikers were charged a fee of one dollar (about four dollars in today's dollars) and were limited to only one night in each shelter. Of course, this meant that PATC had to make sure that it had volunteers who could be at the shelters every weekend during hiking season—no mean feat for a volunteer club located as much as a three-hour drive away from the shelters in the southern end of the park. This compromise system worked well enough that by the following year, there were seven shelters open in the park along the AT, and within a few more years, the monitor system fell by the wayside altogether.

Hikers were not impressed by the park's rules and regulations. Here are just three examples from the shelter register at the Tom Floyd Wayside, the first shelter north of the park, in 1980:

> *"Ah, it's nice to be out of SNP. The regulations made sense but were still a pain. Tonight, I think I'll camp right smack on the trail and love every minute of it!"*

> *"Goodbye SNP. You were fun but fuck your list of rules 10 feet long."*

> *"The park rangers were* [jerks] *because I got a violation for sleeping too close to the trail. It would be a lot better if they didn't have so many rules."*

Within a few years, though, the easing of those rigid rules and the rather in-your-face way they were enforced by park staff meant that hiker unhappiness with the park largely abated. Mostly, though, hikers loved (and still love) stopping at and/or sleeping at one of the trail shelters. Here are just a few examples from shelter registers over the decades:

> *In such a way do I rationalize my love for the beauty, solace, and companionship I find in Nature. May I ever be close to Nature, or may I come upon good people; but may I be especially good to all.*
>
> *—New Hampshire, 1972*

> *I had mixed feelings about a camping trip with 4 kids and 2 adults but it's so beautiful here I'm happy that we came. The wildflowers are each lovely and sometimes exquisite.*
>
> *—Virginia, 1981*

> *This shelter is a great reminder that I never should have gone so long without* [nature].
>
> *—Georgia, 1994*

In the early decades of the Appalachian Trail, so few people hiked in many sections that there was rarely a problem with space at the shelters. But as the number of backpackers grew in the 1960s and then mushroomed after the 1970s, pressure on the shelters and the environment around them grew as well. When thru hiking started to become something that more and more people attempted, a new controversy arose about the use of the trail shelters. Entries in the registers offer evidence that many thru hikers were under the misapprehension that the trail shelters were reserved solely for their use. When thru hikers arrived at a shelter to find it full of a family group, a group of Scouts, a church group or just several weekend hikers, words were sometimes exchanged, which took some of the joy out of the hiking experience for everyone. Some of those thru hikers took to the shelter registers to complain about the presence of other hikers at the shelters: "And we thought this was a haven for through hikers?" Not all thru hikers complained, of course, and many were very happy to meet or greet other hikers on the trail. In all my years of hiking on the AT, the

Boy Scouts on the trail near Deep Gap, Georgia, 1961. *Appalachian Trail Conservancy Archives.*

only time I've ever seen anyone get especially testy with other hikers was when a young couple had their tent set up *inside* the shelter. A group of long-distance hikers arrived—I don't know if they were thru hikers, but they had the look and the smell—and they were very direct with the couple about their bad trail manners.

Plenty of other hiking trails in the United States include trail shelters, many of them Adirondack-style lean-tos like the ones on the Appalachian Trail. But with more than 250 shelters from Georgia to Maine, the AT is certainly unique in the popularity of its shelters. As Jason Miller put it, the shelters have become central nodes in an ephemeral community of hikers who connect, however briefly, at and around those simple wooden structures. They arrive with many purposes—needing a place to sleep, wanting a place to have a picnic, just needing some water or perhaps to use the privy—but they also meet other hikers, read the notes in the register and have a chance to reflect on the beauty of the natural world around them. Sometimes they make friendships that last a few hours. Sometimes those friendships last for years, even decades. But most importantly, they feel a sense of community with other hikers, which is something few other hiking trails offer.

TIME TO EAT

When living in the open air the appetite is so good, and the pleasure of getting your own meals is so great, that, whatever may be cooked, it is excellent.

—*John M. Gould,* How to Camp Out, *1877*

A word on menus: living on pepperoni and pop tarts don't hack it.

—*Maryland, 1984*

When was the last time you ate an onion sandwich? You know, two slices of bread with a little butter spread on them and a nice thick slice of onion in between? If you haven't ever had an onion sandwich, you probably weren't hiking on the Appalachian Trail before the 1950s because in the early decades of the AT, onion sandwiches were one of the staples of the hiker's and backpacker's menu. I'll admit that I recoiled in horror at the idea of an onion sandwich, but the more accounts I've read of hiking the trail in the old days and the more references to onion sandwiches I saw, the more I wondered, "Could they be that bad?" In the interest of historical accuracy, I decided I had to at least try one. So, I did. I took two slices of bread, spread some butter on them and added a slice of a nice, fresh sweet onion. I can now say with confidence that I will never be bringing onion sandwiches on the trail. The whole experience left a bad taste in my mouth—quite literally.

Today's hiker eats a much more diverse menu of foods, both because there are so many more choices available and because American eating habits have diversified significantly since the 1950s. There are, of course, substantial differences in the ways hikers eat depending on whether they are out for the day, are backpacking for a few nights or are on a long-distance journey on the trail. Day hikers and short-distance hikers generally have more options for the simple reason that they don't have to be as concerned about the weight of their food and because they are not reliant on what is available in the small stores that dot the trail's route. The day hiker might carry only snacks or perhaps a sandwich and some fruit. Short-distance backpackers can and often do choose to eat like long-distance hikers, sacrificing taste and nutrition for low pack weights. But just as often, they heed the advice found in various outdoor magazines and online and bring along the fixings for almost gourmet meals. In my many section hikes over the years, I've been known to eat nothing but dehydrated or freeze-dried meals or to go more gourmet (at least for my first night out), making dishes such as beef Bourguignon or Moroccan chicken at a trail shelter.

Hikers have always, always been obsessed with eating for the simple reason that they burn a lot of calories when they're hiking. It's no wonder they think a lot about food while they walk. If they are long-distance hikers, they walk so many miles and burn so many calories that it becomes all but impossible for them to eat enough to just keep up with their calorie burn rate. For these hikers, food becomes more than an obsession—it is an essential aspect of their hiking plan. Over the past one hundred years, what and how hikers eat on the trail has changed almost as much as the gear they carry. Before the Second World War, Appalachian Trail hikers actually ate pretty nutritious meals. They were a pain to cook and weighed far too much, but they were mostly *good for you*. By and large, those early hikers carried lots of fresh fruits and vegetables—onions, carrots, potatoes, apples, peaches in season, plus dried (often referred to in old hiking guides as "desiccated") peas, corn, apricots, raisins and on and on. By the 1960s, the diet of hikers who were spending more than a few nights on the trail became less and less nutritious—in the sense of providing a balanced diet—and more focused on being light and calorie-dense. As the popularity of backpacking grew, more companies began producing and marketing meals and snacks that met those twin requirements.

For decades, Appalachian Trail hikers cooked real meals with diverse and fresh ingredients—meals that smelled good, tasted good and were (mostly) good for them. Of course, they had to cook those meals over fires, which

Cooking dinner along the Appalachian Trail in Maryland, 1939. *Appalachian Trail Conservancy Archives.*

meant they had to know how to build a fire in all weather conditions. They had to find dry wood and enough of it to cook what they wanted when they wanted, and to help with that fire preparation, they had to carry axes, usually short-handled axes clipped to their belts that weighed between one and a half and two pounds. They also had to carry a pan or two to cook all that food in, and they not only had to clean the inside of the pan when they were done but also get all the soot from the fire off the outside of the pan. But they made cornbread. They made stew. They made biscuits. They made "dynamite soup." They generally ate well, and those pans could double as "bear announcers" at the shelters where they slept.

Of course, all that food and cooking gear could weigh a lot. As we've already seen, long-distance hikers in the trail's early decades regularly carried fifty-pound packs, with a lot of that weight coming from their cooking gear and their food. That much weight was an effective bar to entry for the average person, who might not have had the upper body strength to carry that much up and down mountains all day long, which helps to explain why backpackers increasingly tried every strategy they

"Bear announcer" at a trail shelter in the Great Smoky Mountains National Park, 1941. *Appalachian Trail Conservancy Archives.*

could think of to cut down on their pack weight. One thing that helped, though, was that before 1960, most people who hiked on the Appalachian Trail hiked in groups, and group members could share the weight of the cooking gear and, to some extent, the food. A group only needed one axe, not one per person. A group needed slightly larger pots and pans, but those, too, could be shared among the group members. Quite often those group hikes went from a drop-off point to a designated campsite where other club members were waiting with fires burning, pots of stew bubbling away and tables set out with all the fixings. When that happened, hikers only had to carry what they wanted for lunch or snacks and could leave the slabs of bacon and bags of flour with the cooks at camp.

By the second decade after the war, the growing availability of dehydrated and freeze-dried foods, combined with a growing number of camp stove options, meant that backpackers on the trail no longer needed to rely on the support of a group. Those lower pack weights were one of several important factors fueling the rise of backpacking—especially backpacking alone or in pairs or small groups. By the 1960s, hikers of all types—short-distance and long-distance—were able to avail themselves of a growing variety of convenience snack foods to help fuel their hikes. The first Slim Jim meat sticks wrapped in plastic (as opposed to being stored in jars of oil) hit store shelves in the early 1950s. The first Pop-Tart (they were unfrosted) arrived in stores in 1964. The first granola bar appeared on grocery store shelves in the middle of the 1970s. Several other staples of the hiker's and backpacker's menu have been around much longer, including the famous Vienna Sausages packed in their little can, which first appeared in 1903. What made the Vienna Sausage an iconic Appalachian Trail food source? The legendary hiker Grandma Gatewood subsisted largely on those little canned tubes of meat when she couldn't cadge a meal from someone she met along the way. Although peanut butter in the form we know it today had

Breakfast by the campfire along the trail in Tennessee, 1940. *University of Tennessee Archives.*

been around well before the AT appeared on maps, the first wide-mouthed jars so typical on grocery store shelves today appeared in the early 1930s. World War II marked the beginning of peanut butter as a popular product because the U.S. Army used peanut butter heavily in its field rations, and with meat rationing at home, American consumers were encouraged to substitute peanut butter for meat as a source of protein in their diets. Hikers loved the caloric density of peanut butter, and it has been a staple for hikers of all types for more than seventy-five years.

To provide a sense of what AT hikers *did* eat before the days of mass-marketed, freeze-dried meals, here are a few "grub lists" from the 1930s and the 1950s. The first of these is a recommendation for what two backpackers should carry for ten days on the trail in Maine in the 1930s. These days, it's worth remembering that almost no Appalachian Trail hiker would even think about carrying ten days' worth of food for the simple reason that, with the possible exception of the 100 Mile Wilderness in Maine, it's just not necessary. There are now so many small stores along or close to the AT that backpackers rarely need to pack more than five days' worth of food, much less ten. But before the 1960s, few stores stocked what hikers needed, so they had to bring enough grub for however long they were going to be on the trail and then hope for the best when they did go into town. Here, then, is that recommended packing list for two hikers planning to spend ten days on the trail in Maine:

Meat, Eggs, Dairy
5 pounds of bacon
3 pounds of ham
1 pound of dried beef
8 ounces of powdered eggs
2 pounds of canned cheese
1 pound of powdered milk
8 ounces of Crisco
8 bouillon cubes

Vegetables, Fruits, Beans
8 ounces of desiccated potatoes
1 pound of dehydrated vegetables
8 ounces of dried Navy beans
1½ pounds dried apples
1 pound of dried apricots
1½ pounds of raisins
2½ pounds of rice

Baking
7 pounds of flour
3 pounds of cornmeal
4 ounces of baking powder
2 pounds of chocolate
2 pounds of oatmeal
6 pounds of sugar

Other
1 pound of coffee
4 ounces of tea
8 ounces of salt and pepper

That's a lot of food weight, and it doesn't even include the weight of a large frying pan, a coffee pot, some sort of stew pot and at least a large spoon, if not also a metal spatula, for cooking all that food. In other words, this grub list likely required as much as four to six pounds of additional gear just for the cooking. The weight of all that food works out to around two and a half pounds of food per person per day, or twenty-five pounds of food each for ten days on the trail, plus another two or three pounds of cooking gear each. When the short-handled axe is included, these two hikers were carrying almost thirty pounds of food-related provisions and gear for their ten-day trek.

What did they cook with all that food? Typically, backpackers in the early days of the AT would start their day by lighting a fire, and once it had burned down sufficiently to create a nice bed of coals, they would bake either biscuits or cornbread, which they ate with reconstituted eggs and some of that bacon. Lunch was most commonly just handfuls of dried fruit and jerky along the trail, or perhaps an onion sandwich. Dinner, like breakfast, required a fire, and over that fire, they would assemble a soup or a stew from those calorie-dense beans and meat, along with vegetables and rice. Many of the grub lists one finds in the archives include whatever fresh fruits and vegetables hikers could find in season at a store or a farm on the way to or near the trail. But most hikers seemed to rely on biscuits and bacon for breakfast and some sort of stew or soup for dinner. Candy bars were also a common addition to the packing lists, as were peppermints, candied ginger and, by the late 1940s, powdered pudding mix.

Here's another example of a packing list for two hikers, this one from the late 1950s, that relies more on fresh foods and more prepackaged, albeit canned, products:

Meat, Eggs, Dairy
4 Cans of Corned Beef
4 Cans College Inn Chicken a-la-King
6 Pounds of bacon
1 Large can Klim dried milk
10 Erbswurst

Vegetables, Fruits, Beans
2 Pounds of raisins
4 pounds dried apricots
6 pounds of rice
1 pound dehydrated vegetables
3 large onions
4 green peppers

Baking
4 pounds self-rising flour
3 pounds of baker's chocolate
3 pounds of brown sugar

Other
8 ounces of tea

A few of the items on that list required some further research or at least careful thinking. For example, it should have been obvious to me that "Klim" was just "milk" spelled backward. Klim powdered milk was one of the more popular brands available at the time and shows up again and again in packing recommendations. The biggest puzzle, though, involved Erbswurst. It came up over and over as the central ingredient in something hikers called "dynamite soup." First invented in Prussia in the 1860s, Erbswurst was a sausage made from a mixture of pea flower (green or yellow), pork or beef fat, onions and some spices. It quickly became a staple in the Prussian and later German armed forces because it was easy to carry and relatively light and could be sliced up and tossed into some boiling water to make soup at a moment's notice. In the 1880s, the Knorr company, whose products are pretty ubiquitous on the AT these days, began making Erbswurst for the masses, and over time it became a staple of hikers and mountaineers as well as German soldiers. Sadly, in 2018, Knorr declared that due to lack of demand it was discontinuing the product, and Erbswurst became a thing of the Appalachian Trail's past.

But dynamite soup? It just kept cropping up in hiker journals and packing/cooking suggestions, but no matter where I looked, I couldn't find any recipe for it or any description of what seemed to be such a common menu item

Advertisement for Knorr's Erbswurst, circa 1920. *Internet Archive.*

for backpackers. Hiker cookbooks made no reference to dynamite soup, nor did old-timey cookbooks from small towns in Appalachia. If you've ever done archival research, you know that mysteries like this can be like a small rock in your shoe—not so painful that you stop and take your shoe off, but persistently annoying. Finally, in 2019, I found the explanation I'd been looking for—and not because I was still trying to find out what dynamite soup was. Instead, I was reading through the correspondence of members of the Smoky Mountains Hiking Club from the 1930s, and there it was in one of their letters:

> *One of our mainstays is* [a] *soup or stew that is not always above suspicion. With a basis of a handful of rice we add any dehydro vegetables in sight, especially onions, and a stick of Erbswurst, also known from its appearance and its (later) explosive qualities, as dynamite soup—with a little slab of chopped bacon and anything else that is lying around camp. While a stick of Erbswurst alone is supposed to make six plates of delicious soup—the label says so—that's too thin and the mess outlined above will serve just about three or four.*

The soup was "dynamite" because it was so gas-inducing. Given what I know about hiker humor, perhaps that should have been obvious from the start.

No matter what was on those old packing suggestions, one thing seemed to always be there: bacon. When I first saw bacon in the various grub lists I found in the archives, I was of two minds. For bacon eaters like me, there are few smells more inviting than a few slices of the stuff sizzling in a pan. But that smell can be both pervasive and invasive, and if the goal is to reduce the likelihood that a bear will visit your tent or shelter in the night, not having the smell of bacon on one's clothes is probably a good idea. Then there was the matter of the grease. Bacon is just incredibly messy, especially in warmer months, when it tends to release much of its fat onto pretty much anything that is in harm's way. It turns out that backpackers kept all that grease off their gear, their clothes or whatever they had with them by using something called a "pork bag," which could be purchased from Abercrombie & Fitch. As one of its catalogues from the 1930s says, "The pork bags are excellent for carrying pork, bacon, etc., as the material is grease-proof and there is no danger of injury to other articles in the pack." They were nine-by-twelve, weighed six ounces and were priced at fifty cents. That useful product was available at least into the 1950s, which meant hikers could carry bacon

Advertisement for Swift's Premium Bacon, circa 1930s. *Internet Archive*.

with them without fear of turning their packs into greasy, smelly messes. Beginning in 1968, the pork bag was no longer necessary because the DuPont Corporation began marketing a new invention: the Ziploc plastic bag, which hikers have been relying on ever since. But bacon? It's been a while since I last caught the scent of frying bacon near a trail shelter.

Backpackers on the AT in the 1930s and the 1940s didn't always lug slabs of bacon with them. Some could be downright modern in their attempts to pack as light as possible while still maintaining an interesting and healthy diet. For example, one group of hikers who traversed the entire AT in the Smokies in 1941 described their eating this way:

> *Referring to provisions, extensive use was made of dehydrated foods, making it possible to provide interesting menus and healthful meals at the exceptionally light weight of one pound per person per day. Dehydrated versions of potatoes, vegetables, milk, eggs, and fruit were obtained locally at very reasonable prices and they, with a very limited amount of canned meat and fish, formed the piece de resistance of our diet. After experimenting at some length with these foods we were amazed at the variety they offered. During the entire trip we found the meals always appetizing and interesting, and we enjoyed the best of health. Shredded potatoes are lightweight and easily prepared and are excellent, especially when served with powdered gravy.... Cheese omelets, cheese potato cakes, and pancakes were interesting variants. When once the art is mastered, omelets from dried eggs are clever alternatives for cereal breakfasts. Enjoying an omelet on the tenth day of our trip prepared from one-tenth of a pound of carried weight was indeed a novelty to us.*

Eating on the Appalachian Trail began to change significantly after 1945. The Second World War was a turning point for backpacking and hiking in so many ways—new gear, new boots, new foods and new ways to prepare those foods. The decade of the 1950s was also kind of a golden age of processed and packaged convenience foods. Hikers began carrying Jello, Fig Newtons, peanut butter, canned tuna and, increasingly, dried or dehydrated meals and products from companies like Lipton, General Foods and others that they could purchase in local grocery stores. In 1951, a Girl Scout leader in California named Ann Benedict founded Dri-Lite Foods, the first lightweight backpacking meal company in America. Apparently, Benedict got tired of watching her Girl Scouts struggle with heavy cans of beans, tuna and stews during their hikes in the Sierras and began dehydrating meals in

Advertisement for Dri-Lite Foods backpacking meals, circa 1950s. *Internet Archive.*

her garage, first for her Scouts and then for the market. For twenty years, Dri-Lite remained one of the pioneers in the market and was eventually acquired by American Outdoor Products, which began marketing those meals under the brand Backpacker's Pantry. It's a little hard to learn much about Dri-Lite, but Benedict's original trademark application from 1953 says the "Goods and Services" provided under the Dri-Lite name included:

> *Foods in their natural form—namely, cookies; biscuits; candy bars; jelly; nuts; hard candy; dehydrated foods—namely, fruits; applesauce; juice; juice crystals; prepared egg dishes including omelets; pancake mix; syrup for food purposes; oatmeal; cake mix; biscuit mix; bread mix; soups; meats; seafoods; main dish combinations–namely, Spanish rice, chili and beans, meat stew, nonmeat stew, macaroni and cheese, chicken and dumplings, creamed chicken with noodles, chicken and rice, beef stroganoff, beef and potatoes, ham and potatoes; vegetables; salads comprising mixed vegetables in a gelatin and mixed fruits in a gelatin; desserts—namely, pudding with milk, gingerbread, fruit cobbler, cake, pie; imitation ham bits; food beverages—namely, malted milks, non-alcoholic eggnog, and milk.*

In other words, Ann Benedict planned to provide the hiking and camping world with all the delicious meals one could want by just adding boiling water. Dri-Lite's success encouraged several new companies to try their hand at lightweight backpacker meals, including Mountain House, Kampack and Richmor. These days, the number of companies offering freeze-dried or dehydrated backpacking meals seems to grow with each passing year, and the number and variety of meals available to hikers is almost overwhelming.

While Dri-Lite Foods was creating meals specifically for campers and backpackers, after the war the number of quick and easy-to-prepare food options exploded. In addition to Slim Jims, Pop-Tarts, instant oatmeal, granola bars and their kin, other tasty treats worked their way into the hiker menu. When Gene Espy hiked the entire Appalachian Trail in 1951, becoming the second person to hike from Georgia to Maine in one season, one of his staple foods was chocolate pudding:

> *My favorite breakfast included chocolate pudding. I would cook it after supper and let it cool during the night by putting the covered boiler in a spring. After animals tried to get to the pudding I learned to keep it inside my tent overnight and it was fine in the morning.*

When it came to instant pudding, Gene had *many* brands he could choose from and purchase in stores along the trail. Instant pudding had been around since at least 1918, but it wasn't the kind of "instant" that hikers wanted because it still required cooking. But by the time Gene started on his hike, there were several truly instant pudding products already on store shelves across America. Perhaps the first of these was Amazo pudding from American Maize Products, which only required water, something to shake the mix up in and sufficient patience to wait for the pudding to set up. To keep consumers entertained while they waited for their Chocolate Amazo to harden into pudding, each package also contained a card with an "Amazo the Great Magic Trick. Endorsed by Melbourne Christopher, America's Foremost Magician." Amazo Foods was just one of the many brands available to hikers with a taste for pudding. They could choose from Jell-Well, Royal "Shake-a-Pudd'n," perhaps a Puddin' Head Instant Pudding Treat or Jell-O's version that eventually pushed all the others out of the market. For hikers, though, the Jell-O version was much less ideal because it came in a plastic cup that then had to be disposed of properly, which might mean carrying that cup for days.

Advertisement for Amazo Instant Pudding, circa 1950. *Internet Archive.*

By 1950, backpackers also had access to a much wider variety of packaged foods to choose from. While many of those packaged foods of the 1940s and 1950s were packed in cans, it is entertaining to read what was on offer. For example, one catalogue from 1953 offered cans of "broiled hamburgers in tomato and mushroom sauce" (four burgers, price $0.65) or a can of powdered eggs equivalent to eighteen eggs for $1.29. One of the more popular easy meals for backpackers today is Kraft macaroni and cheese. In 1953, that same Kraft macaroni and cheese came in ten-ounce cans for $0.53. What did Appalachian Trail hikers do with all those leftover cans? If they were camped at a trail shelter, they were asked to burn them before departing. Many, if not most, trail shelters in the 1950s had "burn pits" close by where hikers were supposed to burn up their trash, including the cans. Other companies like Kampack, Richmor, Mountain House, Dri-Lite and Backpacker's Pantry offered their products in foil and eventually other forms of packaging that could be more easily disposed of. As those meals began to catch on, the companies realized that the one thing backpackers wanted the most was the ability to just pour their boiling water directly into the package, thereby mitigating the need for a cooking pot to hang over the fire. With so many easy-to-prepare and easy-to-eat options to choose from, backpackers, especially long-distance hikers, all but stopped making biscuits and dynamite soup.

Because making those prepackaged meals required nothing more than boiling water, hikers began to turn to portable stoves rather than open fires to cook their food. What we think of as backpacking stoves have been around much longer than you might imagine. In 1892, F.W. Lindqvist, the inventor of the blowtorch, and his partner, J.V. Svenson, built the world's first portable pressurized kerosene stove in Stockholm, Sweden. Because it was the first, they named it the "Primus" (naturally). Serious adventurers knew all about these new stoves and relied on them as they went into the wild. Roald Amundsen's 1911 expedition to the South Pole used Primus stoves, and in 1953, Tenzing Norgay and Edmund Hillary carried a Primus with them on their historic climb of Mount Everest. At the request of the U.S. Army, the Coleman company developed what became known as the GI Pocket Stove in 1942, and in 1953, another Swedish company announced the SVEA 123, a self-pressurizing portable stove burning white gas. I am partial to the SVEA 123 because it was my first backpacking stove, purchased sometime in the early 1970s. As evidence of its resilience, that old stove from the 1970s still works just fine, and I sometimes take it with me on shorter section hikes. In 1973, Mountain Safety Research, now known just as MSR,

Advertisement for Optimus propane backpacking stove, circa 1980. *Author's collection.*

introduced its Model 9. Today's MSR Whisperlite stove doesn't look much different than that original model. The earliest stoves burned a variety of fuels. Today's hiker relies primarily on small cans of propane, white gas or denatured alcohol. Not having a stove and not being able to build a fire in bad weather could really ruin someone's hike:

> *Feeling pretty down right now. Spent the night here last night,* [it's] *been raining + snow + mixture for 3 days....Most of my stuff is wet including my bag. I do have some dry clothes but they are probably wet now. Also, my feet are killing me and I'm worried that 2 of my blisters might be infected. By the way, I am trying to hike without a stove or a tent to speak of because I am carrying so much food. Was unable to start a fire last night, ate cold beef stew and gorp. If I sound pessimistic right now, I am....At least I still have a positive mental attitude!*
>
> —*Virginia, 1985*

Along with lightweight stoves came lightweight pots and pans. Where the original cooking kits carried by Appalachian Trail backpackers could weigh up to two pounds (or more) and were made from steel or heavy-gauge tin, aluminum cookware was also available and used by many AT hikers. Already in the 1950s, a growing number of companies were offering versions of the nested cooking pots that are commonly available today, and they weren't that much heavier than what you might purchase from a backpacking supplier in 2025. For example, a catalogue from the early 1950s offers several different versions of these nested kits, including a "Rover" set imported from Britain that consisted of two frying pans and a pot for boiling water. When you nested them together, they measured just eight inches wide by four inches high and weighed twelve ounces. If you ditched one of the two frying pans, the weight must have dropped to closer to eight ounces. The entire kit could be yours for $3.95, or about $50 in today's dollars.

These two innovations—lightweight portable cooking stoves with their attendant lightweight pots and pans and prepackaged freeze-dried or dehydrated meals—helped revolutionize backpacking. No longer were hikers dependent on having the skills to get a fire going in all weather conditions. In the early days of the trail, if it was raining or too windy, they just ate their food raw, which they could do because they carried so much fresh food. Portable stoves meant hikers could cook in virtually any weather as long as they could shield their gear from strong winds. Those stoves were also a real boon to the environment along the AT. The relatively small number of hikers on the trail until the 1960s meant that locating sufficient firewood for a cooking fire near a trail shelter was not a difficult task. But with the rapid growth in the hiking population after the 1960s, and the propensity of those hikers to stop for the night at a trail shelter, firewood became more and more difficult to find. Today, it's all but impossible to find sufficient downed wood for a fire anywhere near some of the popular trail shelters, and one can see plenty of evidence of hikers cutting live trees in the mistaken belief that they will be able to build a cheery fire for the night with green wood. The availability of stoves also meant that when hikers did not stay at or near a shelter, they were much less likely to build a fire where they were. Campfires do substantial damage to the ecosystem and significantly increase the risk of forest fires. Portable stoves do neither.

Just as important for the expansion of backpacking as a popular activity was the fact that lighter food and lighter gear meant that many more hikers could imagine themselves slinging on a pack and heading up a mountain or ridge. The advent of light food and light gear took as much as ten pounds off the base weight of the average backpack at the start of a hike, and this meant that hikers in less robust physical condition could venture into the mountains for a few nights or more without feeling dragged to the ground by their gear and their food. No hiker had to have fire-making skills, and food could be cooked in almost all weather conditions, meaning that even in the rain or snow, it was possible to have a hot meal before curling up inside your sleeping bag. In other words, hiking became a lot more fun.

DANGER!

There is an elemental need for a frontier outlet, for a pioneer place to go.
—John McPhee, Coming Into the Country, *1976*

We are all pilgrims. Pioneers. Pathmakers. Don't believe the lie that there are no more frontiers. We of the trail see them every day, for they are within us.
—anonymous AT hiker, Tennessee, 1981

Going on a hike in the mountains means being willing to take risks, and in some ways, the very existence of those risks is part of what makes hiking attractive. From the hikers in the late nineteenth century who wanted to leave behind their middle-class comforts for a few hours, or a few days, to the hikers of the twenty-first century who want to get some exercise, some fresh air and, frankly, to leave behind their comforts for a while, all those hikers saw the mountains as a place to achieve their goals. But they all also wanted to touch the wild, and touching the wild has always meant being okay with some elevated level of risk—risk that makes the experience that much more meaningful. While the Appalachian Trail, with a few notable exceptions, is not an especially risky place to hike, it was and remains a wild place, at least when compared to the neighborhoods hikers come from, and wild places contain their share of dangers. Part of what makes the AT so attractive to so many hikers is the fact that while the trail is a wild place, it's not *that* wild. The wildlife you can meet *can* be dangerous, but mostly it's not. The weather *can* be dangerous, but mostly it's not. There *are* cliffs you could fall off, but only if you are pretty careless.

Many of the things that can make a good hike on the Appalachian Trail go bad in a hurry are gifts to us from the natural world. These include run-ins with plants that don't like us, such as poison ivy, poison oak or stinging nettles. Insects can make us miserable—bees sting, spiders bite and all manner of other insects—including mosquitos, black flies, deer flies, horseflies and what one hiker in the 1940s called "pestiferous chiggers"—want a few drops of our blood. Perhaps worst of all are the several varieties of tick that lurk along the trail, some of which carry Lyme and others of which carry the thankfully rare pathogens that cause really bad things like Rocky Mountain spotted fever, ehrlichiosis, babesiosis and anaplasmosis. Drinking unfiltered, untreated or unboiled water along the trail is just asking to acquire giardia or a chloroform bacterial infection, and there are several reptiles with bad attitudes—the timber and diamondback rattlesnake and the copperhead. Fortunately, all these dangers can be avoided with some preparation and care, and none of them (except for a few very tick-borne pathogens) is life-threatening. But none of them is fun.

There are also mammals that it's better to avoid. Feral hogs in the South are generally not aggressive toward humans but still can be frightening. Moose in the North should be avoided at all costs. Skunks do spray the occasional hiker. Porcupines, mice, chipmunks and raccoons will happily rip a hole in a backpack or a tent to get at human food. And then there are the bears. No other animal seems to engender more worry and consternation among hikers, or at least among the friends and parents of hikers, than bears. One of the most common questions Appalachian Trail hikers get when they tell friends and family they are headed to the trail is, "Aren't you worried about bears?" Perhaps the most famous of all Appalachian Trail hikers—when it comes to worrying about bears, that is—was Bill Bryson. As he was preparing for his attempt at a thru hike of the trail, Bryson obsessed about the possibility of being killed and eaten by a bear:

> *Black bears rarely attack. But here's the thing. Sometimes they do. All bears are agile, cunning, and immensely strong, and they are always hungry. If they want to kill you and eat you, they can, and pretty much whenever they want. That doesn't happen often, but—and here's the absolutely salient point—once would be enough.*

Bears are large and unpredictable and are determined foragers for human food or anything that might smell like food, and in grizzly country, they pose an actual threat to human life. Fortunately for AT hikers, Bill Bryson's anxieties notwithstanding, the Eastern black bear is no grizzly bear. Unlike their Western kin, Eastern black bears are not apex predators and don't see humans as lunch. Since the founding of the Appalachian Trail, only seven people have been killed by black bears in one of the states the trail passes through (not counting those killed by captive bears), and only five of those who died were anywhere near the AT. Interstate 81 is one of the main highways hikers use to access much of the central Appalachian Trail, and in 2023, eight people died on that highway in Pennsylvania alone. But somehow, coming face to face with a bear on a mountain trail just seems more dangerous because the bear is a wild and unpredictable animal.

Of course, bears do sometimes approach humans, and while data on aggressive bear-human encounters is more difficult to come by, there are likely more than ten thousand black bears living within walking distance of the Appalachian Trail; almost all of those bears are keenly interested in what's in your pack, especially if there might be something that is or smells like food. When bears come looking for hikers' food, that can sometimes result in a frightening encounter for both parties and *sometimes* in injuries to the humans. Wildlife managers regularly say that the largest number of such human-bear encounters occur in our national parks—the Smokies and Shenandoah being the relevant case for AT hikers—in large part because those parks are among the most visited by humans (the Great Smoky Mountains National Park is *the* most visited national park) and because they have picnic grounds and campgrounds and restaurants/stores with dumpsters where bears can often find food. But worst of all is the fact that humans seem unable to resist putting out food for bears, especially on picnic tables, so they (the humans) can get a cute photograph of the bear eating their fried chicken or deviled eggs. One might be tempted to think that baiting bears in this way is a more modern human behavior or something that only clueless picnickers do, but Appalachian Trail hikers can be just as clueless. For example, during a 1945 section hike in the Smokies, two AT hikers reported to the ATC:

> *We took a bus to Newfound Gap in the Smokies and spent the night on Mt. Kephart. We had been warned to hang our food out of reach of prowling bears, but though we left a little out for bait, no bears were seen or heard on the trip.*

In fact, just like picnic areas in the national parks, Appalachian Trail shelters quickly became areas of great interest to bears. As more and more humans

Black bear on the Appalachian Trail in Shenandoah National Park, 2014. *Photograph by the author.*

began staying at those shelters, there were more and more interesting things to smell and, if you were a bear, to taste. While many AT shelters these days have bear boxes or bear poles, in those early decades, they had trash pits. Until at least the 1960s, AT hikers often had many tin or aluminum cans in their packs (see "Time to Eat" chapter), and most shelters had a burn pit nearby where hikers were supposed to burn their cans, not because it incinerated the cans altogether but because, in burning, all food residue was removed from those cans. Hikers in the 1950s were advised by the ATC that "[t]he long-distance camper can readily burn and flatten his cans and bury them or if he is in a park or forest he can carry them to the next trash receptacle. The one-day or weekend hiker and camper can take his out with him." One of my favorite

Appalachian Trail photos from the 1950s is "The Burning of the Cans" by Bruce H. Katelle, a member of the Smoky Mountains Hiking Club, which shows a group of hikers burning their cans before they departed from a shelter. Presumably, trail club volunteers would go to their shelters once or twice a year to remove the unburnable remnants of those cans that hikers failed to carry out. By the early 1970s, many shelters, especially those close to roads, had become trash dumps. As the photo of the Moreland Gap Shelter (on the next page) in 1974 shows, before the advent of Leave No Trace, hikers felt no compunction about leaving their beer and food cans in large piles next to the shelters, not even bothering to burn them any longer. No wonder bears found those shelters so interesting.

While AT hikers have worried about the possibility of bear encounters since the Appalachian Trail was founded, seeing a bear is the embodiment of wildness and inspires awe, fear, admiration and a sense that one truly has crossed over from civilization to the wild. In one of the most famous passages from his book *Coming Into the Country*, John McPhee described an encounter with a grizzly bear on Alaska's Salmon River. McPhee and several friends were in kayaks on the river, and they came up suddenly on a young bear catching salmon, playing with them and then throwing them aside. While they watched from their kayaks:

> *The bear turned away, bored. He began to move upstream by the edge of the river. Behind his big head his hump projected. His brown fur rippled like a field under wind. He kept coming. The breeze was behind him. He had not yet seen us. He was romping along at an easy walk. As he came closer to us, we drifted slowly toward him. The single Klepper* [kayak], *with John Kaufmann in it, moved up against a snagged stick and broke it off. The snap was light, but enough to stop the bear. Instantly, he was motionless and alert, remaining on his four feet and straining his eyes to see. We drifted toward him. At last, we arrived in his focus. If we were looking at something we had rarely seen before, God help him so was he.*

At that moment, McPhee and his companions sat at the edge of danger, drifting ever closer to an apex predator, and the story could have ended very badly. Instead, the bear turned, climbed the bank and left them to drift past while trying to remember to breathe again.

The typical Appalachian Trail hiker is nowhere near as lyrical as McPhee—few people are or will be—but hikers can still express just how exciting it is to see a bear on the trail for the first time or the one hundredth

"The Burning of the Cans," Tennessee, 1955. *University of Tennessee Archives.*

Trash at the Moreland Gap Shelter, Tennessee, 1974. *Appalachian Trail Conservancy Archives.*

time. In the summer of 1949, trail volunteer John W. Clark was hiking on the AT in the Bigelow Range in Maine for a few days, and he wrote:

> *The next morning, I overslept and the sun was shining brightly before I awakened. As I was working up towards East Peak, I saw something I have always wanted to see but never have—a mother bear and cub. I was sitting on a rock near the junction of the side trail to Old Man's Head, stirring a fresh can of paint, when I saw the two come into the Trail. The mother rolled several old logs over for the cub to eat bugs. When they were within about 30 feet of me, I thought I better let them know I was there. The she-bear took one look and went tearing off up the Trail without even a glance at the cub. The poor cub started after his mother as fast as he could go, yelping just like a puppy that has had its tail stepped on.*

Black bear along the Appalachian Trail in Virginia, 2018. *Photograph by the author.*

Fifteen years later, an unknown hiker writing in the shelter register at the Tom Floyd Wayside just outside the northern boundary of Shenandoah National Park expressed even more excitement at seeing bears on the trail: "SNP was great. I love those CCC trails and all the wildlife. I saw 3 of the 7 bears Leonard saw!" My favorite, though, was a German hiker I met at the Rod Hollow Shelter about a decade ago. When I asked her why she had decided to come all the way from Germany to hike on the Appalachian Trail, she told me, in a thick German accent, "I wanted to see bears. We don't have bears on our trails in Germany." I then asked if she had seen bears since she started her hike in Georgia. "Ja. Twenty-seven. It's too many." Despite seeing too many bears, it was the possibility of those bears and what they meant for being in the "wild" that drew her across the Atlantic to the Appalachian Trail and was probably the thing she talked about the most when she got home.

When it comes to actual danger on the trail, hikers have always been much more likely to run afoul of other animals than bears, venomous snakes in particular. In fact, the history of the Appalachian Trail is quite literally strewn with the carcasses of dead rattlesnakes, copperheads and other snakes that hikers mistook for pit vipers and decided to kill. Killing snakes on a hike was seemingly so common that it's a bit surprising that the ATC never published a "Guide to Killing Snakes" to go along with all its other guidebooks and pamphlets. To be sure, the ATC and many of the trail clubs always encouraged hikers to pack a "Snake Bite Kit" with them in their gear, and the newest innovations in such kits were regularly reviewed in the *Appalachian Trailway News*. But the ATC never advocated the killing of snakes. Instead, hikers just took matters into their own hands:

> *In Pennsylvania everyone seemed concerned about snakes. Much to almost everyone's surprise we saw only one poisonous snake, a copperhead, which we promptly killed.*
>
> —*Virginia, 1950*

> *About three miles from Wallace Gap, ascending Little Bald Mtn., on a switchback, there was a fallen sapling on a portion of the trail which was quite grassy. Rev. Morgan stopped to pick the tree up and we heard the rattle. Although this was the first time I had ever heard a rattlesnake, I knew instinctively what it was and started to retreat. When the snake rattled, Rev. Morgan chopped its head off with the machete, aim quicker than the eye could see!*
>
> —*North Carolina, 1950*

> *A big stick or rock is effective against rattlers (we killed six). And all other creatures are more afraid of you than you are of them.*
>
> *—Owen Allen and Lochlin Gregory, describing their hike in 1961*

> *I killed 15–20 rattlers and 5 copperheads with my hiking staff. This is a chinaberry stick I began carrying when I was 12 years old, so of course it had to make the long trip with me.*
>
> *—Gene Espy, describing his 1951 thru hike*

I met Gene Espy at his home in the summer of 2019, and while I was there, he took that old chinaberry stick from its place of honor on the living room wall and handed it to me to hold. I'll admit that I might have turned it over once or twice to check for snake bloodstains.

It's possible that the desire of so many hikers to eliminate snakes from the Appalachian Trail by force could be seen as a kind of primordial, instinctual drive to eliminate threats to the human species, or the result of religious training and folk tales that cast snakes as evil or as villains. More likely is the fact that until the advent of the environmental movement in the 1960s, most hikers saw nature as something to be used for their benefit—even if using meant killing—rather than as something to try to live in harmony with. While both rattlesnakes and copperheads *can* have bad attitudes when it comes to humans who invade their personal space, if given a wide berth they are no threat at all. Plenty of AT hikers have been bitten by either (or both) of these vipers over the decades, most often because they stepped too close to the snake, but of the many millions of hikers who have set foot on the Appalachian Trail since 1925, so far not one has died from a snakebite. Some have been miserable for days or weeks after being bitten, and many others have just received "dry" bites from the snakes where no venom was injected. Dry bites can be plenty terrifying in the moment, but at least the end result is not nearly as unpleasant. And it also needs to be said that not every AT hiker in the trail's early decades saw snakes as something to be killed:

> *We know that rattlesnakes, for all their evil reputation, have caused about as much harm as a moonbeam.*
>
> *—Harvey Broome, 1948*

With the advent of the modern environmental movement, hikers' attitudes about snakes began to shift, and by the 1980s, the human-snake carnage seems to have largely abated in favor of a more live-and-let-live approach to snakes on the trail. Instead of regaling others with stories of how many snakes they or one of their hiking companions killed, hikers were much more likely to just add warnings about snakes or to just tell stories about meeting them along the trail to their entries in trail shelter register:

> *Warning: Snake in shelter above picnic table in rafter. It's a copperhead.*
>
> *—Virginia, 1980*

> *Yesterday saw two deer, South River Falls, and a rattlesnake by the park boundary. Quite frightening to say the least.*
>
> *—Virginia, 1981*

> *Saw my first diamondback rattlesnake. A little one, sunning itself on a rock beside the trail. A cute little guy, oblivious to the world, until it sensed human presence & then shot into the ground. Too bad—was going to get a picture of it.*
>
> *—Tennessee, 1987*

> *Saw a snake eating a woodchuck. Too late to intervene. Put a grave marker at the site later on.*
>
> *—Pennsylvania, 2004*

But just like bears, venomous snakes bring hikers face to face with the wildness of nature. One look into the vertically split pupils of a viper is more than enough to freeze any hiker in their tracks. Hearing the telltale hissing chatter of a rattler nearby gets the heart racing. Rounding a boulder or tree on the trail and coming suddenly upon one of those slithery denizens of the Appalachian Mountains definitely provides a rush of adrenaline.

Much more likely to kill or just plain injure hikers than either snakes or bears is weather. And even weather is, in the end, not very likely to kill us, although hikers have been struck by lightning from time to time. Perhaps the most spectacular example in recent memory happened in the Maryland section during the summer of 2015. Three hikers took refuge from an approaching thunderstorm in the Washington Monument that sits next to the trail. One moment it was just raining and the next all three were blasted out of the monument by a lightning strike on the structure. They survived, but it was certainly an experience all three hope to never relive. In fact, like snakebites, death by lightning on the AT is incredibly rare, so rare than in one hundred years it seems that only two AT hikers have died from a lightning strike. Much more deadly to hikers, whether they are on the AT or elsewhere, is hypothermia. While we tend to think of hypothermia as a cold-weather problem, rapidly changing weather conditions in the mountains can give a hiker hypothermia in any month of the year. I know because I once got a mild case in Southern Virginia in July. Cold weather, snow, ice and freezing rain can all put hikers at an elevated level of risk on the trail, and over the years, they have. Of course, the weather doesn't have to be a danger for it to ruin a hike, but being cold and wet rarely improves the hiking experience. Ice storms happen all along the trail in the spring and fall, and few sounds are as disconcerting to listen to while lying in your tent than the sharp reports of branches snapping under the weight of the gathering ice or the sudden crashing of a large tree falling nearby.

Humans bring their own pathogens to the Appalachian Trail, and those pathogens can spoil anyone's hike. Over the past few decades, it seems that every year there is an outbreak of norovirus at one of the trail shelters in the South as the "thru hiker bubble" makes its way north from Springer Mountain. In 2016, the outbreak in the North Carolina/Tennessee section of the trail was so bad that some hikers took to calling it "Spewmageddon." One wrote:

> *Well, I've holed up here at the Fontana Dam Lodge for the last two days and now to be third because of Norovirus. It's been brutal and demoralizing. I won't give you gory details but suffice it say I was chugging along the trail at a good pace and now this.*

In addition to norovirus, humans bring along many other contagious viral or bacterial friends, often leaving them behind in trail shelters or, more commonly, in the privies near the shelters or in nearby water sources. A recent study of the springs at or near the trail shelters in the Great Smoky Mountains National Park found that nine out of ten had levels of chloroform bacteria that exceeded the levels found acceptable by the CDC. Drinking unfiltered or untreated water from those springs is just an invitation to illness.

Hikers do get lost along the Appalachian Trail—I did once when I was twelve—but only rarely does getting lost result in a crisis. Almost everywhere on the trail, with a few exceptions in New England, it's enough to walk downhill, find a stream and follow it to the next stream, which eventually will take you to a road and safety. The dense and wilder forests of New England are another story. It's quite possible to become very lost in Vermont, New

Hampshire and Maine—the kind of lost that can lead to serious problems. The part of Grandma Gatewood's story that most people don't know is that at the beginning of her first attempt to hike the AT, she started at Mount Katahdin and, early on, stepped off the trail for a moment and couldn't find her way back. Then she dropped her glasses and stepped on them, making it even more difficult for her to figure out where she was going. When she didn't show up at the next stopping point, local park rangers mobilized search parties to find her. Ultimately, she found them rather than the other way around, and the head ranger put her on a bus and sent her home to Ohio with some not very polite advice. In 2013, thru hiker Geraldine Largey ("Inchworm") made a similar mistake, stepping off the trail in Maine and then not being able to find her way back. Sadly, Largey died before searchers could find her. With millions of people setting foot on the Appalachian Trail every year, it is inevitable that someone will become lost no matter the white blazes and well-worn nature of the footpath. Fortunately, stories like Largey's have been and are incredibly rare.

Of course, hikers do also worry about the possibility of dangerous encounters with other humans. For the first fifty years of the trail's existence, human dangers seemed all but nonexistent, but that sense of safety was shattered in 1974 when an escaped convict murdered hiker Joel Polsom and abducted his female companion (whom he later released). Since that horrible event, only another dozen hikers have been murdered on or near the Appalachian Trail. While each of those events is incredibly tragic, a hiker's odds of being murdered on the Appalachian Trail are statistically about one thousand times less than their odds of being murdered during their daily life elsewhere in America. Lower-level crime does occur on the trail, although historical statistics on such crimes are all but impossible to come by. The *possibility* of a violent crime happening in the forest does deter some from hiking on the trail, but as the first guide to thru hikers said in the 1980s (and is still true today), "You are sadly mistaken about what the AT is and has to benefit you with if you feel the need to pack a gun, a hatchet, and a bowie knife."

Human-caused danger could also come from the trail's proximity to military bases. Until 1950, the trail crossed the Indiantown military reservation in Pennsylvania, but in 1950, the *Appalachian Trailway News* informed hikers that "due to this area now being used for artillery and bombing practice through practically the entire year, it has become necessary to abandon the trail on the Reservation and prohibit its use at any time." Instead, hikers would be required to take an eleven-mile road walk to avoid being bombed or shelled.

The possibility of dangers great and small is always there on the Appalachian Trail, and frankly, it is that possibility that makes any hike in the mountains a bit more exciting. Even if you've hiked the same section of the trail fifty times, you still don't know what's around the next bend. A bear? A fallen tree you'll have to circumnavigate? A footbridge collapsed into a stream overflowing with snowmelt? Two men with long guns staring intently into the upper reaches of a tree? A rattlesnake sunning herself in the middle of the trail? This unpredictability is one of the chief appeals of wilderness hiking. Our twenty-first-century lives have become very predictable and routinized. The trail offers us the promise of the unexpected. Although the Appalachian Trail passes through many wild places and can sometimes take hikers far from civilization and help, the AT remains a safe place for hikers of all types to leave the stresses and cares of daily life behind for a few hours, a few days or for months, with little real danger. But the natural world is not without risk, and it is the existence of that risk that reminds hikers that they are indeed able to experience those wild places they visit as humans always have—with caution and with wonder. The frisson we feel when we hear a large animal walking in the woods near our tent at night, or when we hear the haunting call of a pileated woodpecker on the ridge above us, reminds us that we are alive, that we are human and that we are part of the wild places around us.

FINDING THEIR WAY

Just out for a leisurely day hike, taking my time, just enjoying! Have to go to work this p.m., but I will be in a great frame of mind.

—*Tennessee, 1987*

It was one thing to build a two-thousand-mile trail in the 1920s and the 1930s, but once the trail was underway, hikers needed to know how to get there and, once there, how to navigate their way along the new trail. For this reason, at the same time they were building the trail, the ATC and the trail clubs began writing guides for hikers, putting up signs along roads and at important waypoints along the trail and, perhaps most importantly, marking the trail itself so that hikers would know they were still on the right path. The first guidebooks were incredibly detailed, although the maps included with those guides were all but useless for specific navigation because they lacked much detail. The specificity of those old guides continued through the decades, and only recently have they become less detailed about where to turn, how far to go until the next road crossing and so on. Here's just one example from the 1969 edition of *The Guide to the Appalachian Trail in Maine*, describing the approach to the Saddleback Ranch from the south:

From the dirt road on the old railroad grade along Orbeton Stream, the trail ascends steeply for ⅓ of a mile, then more gradually, climbing toward the dome of Poplar Ridge. The route passes over a rocky section with sparse growth and crosses a brook at 2.3 miles, where the Poplar Ridge Lean-to is

> *located. The trail then bears left, crossing another summit, and then a boggy section, and ascends the south slope of Saddleback Junior, crossing a brook in 3 and ⅓s miles. Just beyond, it emerges from the woods and reaches the summit of Saddleback Junior at 3.62 miles.*

In addition to making the trail more accessible, and easier to navigate, those guidebooks were an important source of revenue for the ATC. It's hard to imagine now given the organization's $15 million annual budget, but until the 1970s, the Appalachian Trail Conference (Conservancy) was perpetually broke. The ATC had only three sources of revenue until the 1970s: membership dues, dues paid by the trail clubs and the sale of guidebooks and maps. The sale of guidebooks was especially important to the Conference's bottom line. The Green Mountain Club and the Appalachian Mountain Club sold their own guidebooks, but Myron Avery wanted hikers to buy the ATC's guides. At one point, Avery got into such a squabble with the AMC over guidebook sales that the leadership of that venerable hiking club almost ditched the AT project altogether. Avery was also forever pushing the local clubs to purchase hundreds of the trail guides from the ATC and then to resell them to club members and local hikers. Sometimes, the local clubs were happy to comply with his pestering. Other times, they politely but firmly refused. When they did, he just became more insistent, sometimes leading to strained relations between the local clubs and the ATC. After Avery's death, the local clubs increasingly wrote and sold their own guides, depriving the ATC of some sales revenue but putting out guides that were a bit more locally focused than the ATC-driven publications had been. Because the clubs also cared for trails other than the Appalachian Trail, they often published guides to those other trails as well, leading to a slew of trail guidebooks sprouting up all along the AT. One of the wonderful features of many of those older guidebooks was that they were bound on metal posts, and hikers could detach the covers, slide the pages and maps they needed off the posts and leave the rest of the book at home. These days, guidebooks are bound, so hikers who don't want the weight have to copy or tear out the pages they want. There aren't many examples of people in the pre-1960s era doing things in a more ecologically friendly way, but the removable page design of those old guides is certainly one.

What those old trail guides offered that is a little harder to come by these days was local expertise. Not long ago, I had the good fortune to meet Jean Golightly, a longtime volunteer with the Potomac Appalachian Trail Club. At the time of our conversation, Jean was ninety years old and still very active and independent. For decades, she had been the main author of the PATC's trail guides along the section of the AT the club was responsible for, and according to Jean, her first guidebooks were written on a typewriter, hand-edited and then typed again. Only in the late 1970s or early 1980s did the club finally invest in one of those new-fangled IBM PCs so she could do her writing and editing in a word processing program. When I spoke with Jean, one of the things I was curious about was her research process. Did she rely on information from other hikers? Or did she gather the trail data herself?

> *I was the hiker. One of the areas that I did was the area around Big Schloss on the Virginia–West Virginia line. It was an area that there was nothing written about at that point, and I found someplace an old Xerox copy of the area that had some lines drawn on it that looked like trails. That's how I explored the area, because there were no other maps available. It was such fun.*

Jean Golightly is just one of hundreds of hikers, authors and researchers who produced guidebooks for other hikers over the decades. Without their tireless efforts, the Appalachian Trail and all the trails in its network would have been so much more difficult to hike. But those trail guides were really wayfinding guides—how to get from Point A to Point B without getting lost. As backpacking really took off as a recreational activity in the 1970s, hikers, especially long-distance hikers, wanted more.

In 1982, Darrell Maret, who went by the trail name "The Philosopher," self-published an ersatz guide to thru hiking the Appalachian Trail. That first version was only 14 pages long and focused mostly on what Maret knew long-distance hikers really wanted to know: namely, where to find cheap hotels in town and, even more important, where the best all-you-can-eat restaurants near the trail were located. Maret's guide caught on, and the following year, the ATC published and distributed a longer (40-page) version. By 1990, *The Philosopher's Guide* had mushroomed to 160 pages—much too long to be carried without ditching something else from your pack. Maret's guidebook became a Bible for long-distance hikers, whether they were attempting to hike the whole trail or were just out for a few weeks. Later iterations of the *Guide* included advice on where to find the best milkshakes or the best pizza and which towns had stores that offered backpacking gear. It was, in short, a compendium of all the things that the official trail guides lacked. Maret published *The Philosopher's Guide* for a number of years, and the success of his guide spawned a small cottage industry in guides to long-distance hiking on the AT. Now, of course, the Internet offers a virtually unlimited number of guides, from books to videos to apps to websites. In 1980, hikers had very little information about how to navigate the entire trail. Today, they have too much.

Among the more popular of the current guides is *The Appalachian Trail Data Book*, which has been compiled for forty years by Daniel Chazin. The *Data Book* is a useful tool for hikers who don't want to rely on apps on their phone to know how far it is from where they are to where they want to go on the trail. Unlike *The Philosopher's Guide*, the *Data Book* was not intended specifically for thru hikers, but rather for anyone who wanted to hike on the Appalachian Trail for however long. If you were a thru hiker, you could just tear out the pages as you went along or ship the relevant pages to yourself in your bounce box so you didn't have to carry the weight. If you were a shorter-distance hiker, you could just tear out (or copy) the pages you needed and stuff them in your pack. What made the *Data Book* especially useful was that it boiled down the trail to its most essential features—how far was it from here to there and where were the water sources, shelters, iconic views and road crossings—and what was the elevation profile of the trail ahead of you. It didn't offer the almost step-by-step directions of the old trail guides, but it did provide the most essential information for hikers.

Because the Appalachian Trail is so well blazed and has so many directional signs all along the trail's route, it's a bit difficult to imagine today that when the trail began one of the most important tasks for the trail club volunteers was to make sure hikers could navigate their way along the footpath. Those early trail builders experimented with a number of different blazing strategies, including a variety of copper and tin markers attached to trees and fence posts, but the metal markers that were first used proved to be far too expensive and far too tempting to hikers who wanted a souvenir of their hike. Ultimately, the ATC and the trail clubs settled on the now-familiar rectangular white blaze seen by millions of hikers every year. Those old galvanized tin markers continued to be employed in some locations for many decades, and if you watch carefully during your hike, you might just see one on the side of a tree, often with the bark beginning to swallow the marker.

During the earliest decades of the trail, many sections, like those in much of the new Shenandoah National Park, crossed open fields with few, if any trees, fence posts or other structural items that might take a sign or a blaze. There are fewer field crossings on the AT today, but there are still plenty and

Myron Avery and Frank Schairer building a cairn on the Appalachian Trail in Virginia, 1932. *Potomac Appalachian Trail Club Archives.*

many of those open fields have weathered wooden posts or thin rectangular plastic posts with the AT blaze on them. But in those first decades, most of those fields still contained livestock, and cows and horses love nothing more than to rub against a signpost until they snap it off. To deal with this problem, the early trail builders often built rock cairns to mark the route of the trail through a pasture, painting a white blaze on the topmost rock to help guide their fellow hikers, especially on foggy days. To help hikers over pasture fences, the trail club volunteers built stiles or complex pass-through gates, many of which are still in use today.

Those white blazes were very helpful, except in the winter months, when snow could obscure them, and in some of the snowier parts of New England, the clubs insisted on using orange paint instead of white. The quality of the trail blazing was not always to every hiker's liking, however, and the shelter registers contain numerous examples of complaints about a perceived lack of proper blazing. Not everyone complained, of course. As one hiker in New Hampshire wrote in response to some negative comments about the state of blazing, "Too bad if the blazing is a little weird at times. Isn't hiking

Sign along the Appalachian Trail in North Carolina, circa 1985. *Appalachian Trail Conservancy Archives.*

supposed to build character? People seem to get here and if they don't, they'll probably run into some of the fine natives."

In addition to marking the trail with blazes and little tin markers, the trail clubs began putting up signs at important points along the trail, giving hikers a sense for how far it was to the next shelter or the next important geographical feature like a river, a summit, a town or the intersection with another trail. These days, those trail signs are generally brown with white lettering either painted onto them or carved into them with a router or woodworking tools and then painted white. At some of the trail clubs, the making of trail signs has gone high tech, but in others, those signs are still made the old-fashioned way, carved by hand by trail club volunteers. Then, as now, keeping those signs in good condition for hikers was a chore for the trail clubs. Bears seemed to love to chew on them, rub against them or just break them, and vandals carved into them, wrote on them or simply stole them. The theft of trail signs at road crossings and trailheads was and continues to be a major headache for trail maintainers and for hikers who rely on those signs for navigation—especially casual hikers/day hikers.

Perhaps the most surprising example of sign stealing was the theft of a very heavy bronze marker placed at the original midpoint of the trail in

Wooden sign on Centerpoint Knob, Pennsylvania, 1935. *Appalachian Trail Conservancy Archives.*

1938. Sometime in the 1940s, that large and very heavy bronze plaque at the summit of Centerpoint Knob in Pennsylvania vanished from the boulder it was bolted to. It was there in 1940 because a photo from that year (see pages 16–17) shows a group of PATC hikers sitting by the plaque. And it was missing in 1948 because Earl Shaffer (the first to hike from Georgia to Maine in one year) took a photo of himself standing next to the boulder and the plaque was gone. That old bronze plaque resurfaced not too long ago when a man laying fence posts on his property near the mountain dug a hole and hit the plaque where the thieves had buried it. He eventually donated it to the Appalachian Trail Museum, and a replica has been reattached to that boulder where the original once lived.

The most famous Appalachian Trail sign of all, though, and the one that every northbound thru hiker dreams about, is the sandwich board sign on the summit of Mount Katahdin. That famous sign was a later addition to the trail. Early hikers on the AT who reached the mountain's summit were greeted instead by a small white sign with black lettering that told them how far it was to the other end of the trail and reminded them to register. Mount Katahdin didn't get its iconic sandwich board sign until the 1960s, when a sign maker named Clyde Smith from the Roan Highlands of Tennessee made the first version of the now iconic sandwich board sign. Ever since, hikers, especially thru hikers, have climbed up on that sign, leaned against it, kissed it, sat on it and gone into a victory pose with it to signify their conquest of the mountain or of the trail.

With the advent of the iPhone in the summer of 2007 and the subsequent roll-out of other data phones, all of which included GPS receivers after 2008, navigating the Appalachian Trail changed dramatically. It took a few years for those new phones to have an impact on hikers because cell service along the trail was so spotty, but once cell towers started popping up near the trail, hikers could suddenly access the Internet from the wilderness. It's probably best that Benton MacKaye didn't live to see this development because he would have been appalled and heartbroken. From his perspective in the 1930s, it was bad enough that hikers on his trail would have to hear cars and motorcycles on Skyline Drive and the Blue Ridge Parkway. Just imagine how he would have felt had he known that now hikers could bring their social media bubble with them on the trail and could listen to music or podcasts or YouTube videos while they hiked, missing entirely the healing sounds of nature? But for hikers of all types navigating the trail, data phones have become so much a part of their lives off the trail that having one on the trail feels almost as essential as having water, some snacks or camping gear. GPS receivers don't rely on cell coverage, which makes it possible to navigate, or at least geolocate, almost anywhere on the trail as long as your phone is charged. That access has meant that shorter-distance hikers generally don't need a guidebook or a map to find their way. By 2024, some publications estimated that as much as 90 percent of the Appalachian Trail has cell coverage, and the all-but-ubiquitous availability of a cell signal on

Wooden sign on the summit of Mount Katahdin, Maine, 1951. *Photograph by Gene Espy, used with permission.*

the trail has led to the development of several apps for hikers that include all the kinds of information one could find in the old trail guides, as well as publications like *The Philosopher's Guide* and the *AT Data Book*. As long as a hiker's phone has a connection and a battery charge, they can find their way north or south, check for the nearest parking lot or road access and even find information about the best pizza nearby. Of course, hikers can also hike whatever portion of the Appalachian Trail they prefer by just getting to the trail and following the white blazes, just as they did in the 1930s or the 1960s or the 1990s.

TRAIL TOWNS, HOTELS, HOSTELS AND TRAIL MAGIC

Into Front Royal again today for Pizza Hut and maybe more beers—God this trail is tough on the spirit.

—*Virginia, 1980*

Hotel in Fayetteville is closed. Stay at the Rite Spot Motel. They will shuttle you to and from Caledonia.

—*Pennsylvania, 2004*

Benton MacKaye wanted the Appalachian Trail to be a wilderness trail, a place where hikers could leave civilization behind for a few hours, a few days or a few weeks to find a peaceful and healing respite from the problems of living in a modern industrial society. In its earliest days, large sections of the AT were certainly that—places where human civilization was only barely evident, and the sounds, smells and sights of nature could overwhelm hikers, crowding out worries about jobs, bills, local politics, global tensions or just about any other stress-inducing aspect of their lives. But the Appalachian Trail was also a town trail, one that passed through and still passes through dozens of towns—places like Hot Springs, North Carolina; Damascus, Virginia; Harpers Ferry, West Virginia; and Hanover, New Hampshire—on its way north and south. In 2022, the National Park Service estimated that the Appalachian Trail crosses a road more than five hundred times, which is surely a significant reduction from the pre–World War II decades for the simple reason that so much of the trail was *on* a

Road walking in the Carlisle Valley, Pennsylvania, 1977. *Appalachian Trail Conservancy Archives.*

road, either paved or unpaved, until the 1980s. While the trail is *mostly* (but not entirely) in the forest these days, it still passes through towns on a very regular basis—generally every three to five days according to the ATC. In other words, the AT is *both* a wilderness trail *and* a town trail, which is one of the many reasons it continues to be so popular.

All that road walking and town hiking made and continues to make the Appalachian Trail accessible to hikers, and for long-distance hikers, regular access to towns means that they can resupply their packs on a regular basis, cutting down on the need to carry seven to ten days' worth of provisions. When you can buy more food or pick up supplies at a local post office every few days, pack weights on a long-distance hike go way down, making longer hikes easier and more attractive to more people. For day hikers, the trail's proximity to towns has meant easy access to trailheads and easy access to meals and snacks after a good day of hiking. Before the 1960s, almost all hikers on the AT were out on the trail for a few hours, days or weeks, and as we saw in the "Time to Eat" chapter, provisioning guides often listed what two hikers would need for ten days on the trail. In the trail's early decades, despite the road and town walking, it was often necessary to carry large amounts of food for the simple reason that the communities along the trail were not organized around the needs of hikers. In fact, until the 1970s, many people who lived in communities along the trail barely knew of the trail's existence, and when they did, they could be quite surprised to meet a backpacker or two ambling down the road into their town or stopping in their local store.

Today, stores in the many little towns that dot the trail's route are well stocked with the foods and supplies hikers want, from energy bars to jerky to peanut butter to moleskin for blistered feet. But in the 1930s, 1940s, 1950s or even into the 1960s and 1970s, hikers who stopped in those stores had to make do with whatever the owners stocked based on the needs and desires of their neighbors, not the needs and desires of hikers. The fact that stores along the trail didn't cater to hikers helps to explain the growing popularity of mailing boxes of supplies to a small-town post office somewhere along the route of a hike that was going to last more than five or six days. Early advice literature about mailing supplies ahead was *very* specific about the need to plan to be at a small-town post office before noon on a Saturday, because after 12:00 p.m. that office might just be closed. When trail names started to become a common aspect of the long-distance hiker experience in the late 1970s, hikers were regularly warned to remember to mail their boxes to themselves, not to "Moonbeam" or "Frodo." Many hikers over the years made that mistake and were turned away when they requested a box addressed to a Tolkien-inspired wanderer.

MacKaye didn't intend the Appalachian Trail to become an economic engine for rural Appalachia, but that is in fact what it has become over the decades. As more and more hikers go to the trail, whether for a day hike or something more, they stop in the little towns nearby to purchase food, gas, ice cream or just about anything else a hiker might want or need. Until fairly recently, the relationship between those towns and the hiker community was very informal, but beginning in 2010, the ATC began designating towns along the trail as official "A.T. Communities." In 2024, there were fifty-six such communities in the network, with more being added each year. The original trail guides and later the ersatz ones like *The Philosopher's Guide* often offered hikers detailed information on where one could buy supplies, especially food, near the trail and, just as importantly, where one could spend the night, whether before, during or after one's hike. Today, AT hikers are served by an ever-expanding network of hotels, motels, hiker hostels and short-term rentals, especially in official AT communities, making it easy for someone to hike for the day but spend the night in a warm bed with easy access to a hot shower and breakfast. It is easy to think of Airbnb and similar businesses as recent innovations, but in the trail's early decades, people who lived along or close to the trail took in hikers as boarders, letting them sleep in barns or bedrooms and offering them meals for a reasonable price and often a bath or a shower—as long as those hikers were White. Hikers of color, of which there were certainly few until the 1980s or 1990s, could not expect the same level of hospitality much of anywhere along the trail.

In 1949, *National Geographic* writer Robert Brown journeyed along the length of the Appalachian Trail with photographer Robert Sisson and subsequently wrote the first story about the trail to reach a truly national audience. Writing about the route of the trail through Southwestern Virginia, Brown told of staying as a boarder at the home of John Barnard, who oversaw the AT in and around the Dan River Gorge. The trail moved away from that part of Virginia in 1952, but when Brown arrived unannounced at Barnard's home that night, he knocked on the front door and was greeted by "a tall man with gentle eyes" who said that, yes, Brown could stay the night. Barnard told his guest to sit a bit on the front porch because he still had chores to do. After a while, Mrs. Barnard invited Brown inside for a dinner any hiker would relish:

> *Bowls of vegetables and stewed fruit, platters of meat, plates piled high with hot biscuits and cornbread, pitchers of milk and cream, jars of honey and homemade jam crowded the table. There was squash, string beans, and mashed potatoes; hot veal and cold ham; applesauce and pears; and quantities of sweet farm fresh butter to slather on the hot breads. What a feast!*

In 2019, I sat on that same front porch, chatting with John Barnard's grandson Ralph about the hikers who came to their farm in the 1930s and the 1940s. Now in his eighties, Ralph was a teenager in those days and shared many happy memories of meeting the hikers, taking them down into the gorge for a day hike and listening to their stories about life in Washington, D.C., and other big cities he'd never visited.

There were also plenty of hotels and motels up and down the trail's route where hikers could spend one or more nights during a hike before they began or after they finished walking. For those White hikers who preferred to sleep under a roof not belonging to a trail shelter, the options were often quite varied, ranging from places like the Lake View Motel in Fancy Gap, Virginia, to the 1896 House in Williamstown, Massachusetts, to the legendary (with hikers) Doyle Hotel in Duncannon, Pennsylvania. In the White Mountains, hikers could pay for a night or two at one of the AMC's high mountain huts, getting a hearty dinner and breakfast as well as a bunk to sleep in.

The Doyle Hotel, Duncannon, Pennsylvania, circa 1965. *Appalachian Trail Conservancy Archives.*

These days, the Appalachian Trail in Maine is considered one of the more challenging sections of the entire trail, especially the famed 100 Mile Wilderness between Monson and Baxter State Park. But when hikers first began venturing onto the AT in Maine even before its completion there in 1937, they found a trail *very* different from the one hikers use today. In 1934, a group of AMC members set out to hike the entire trail in Maine and, except for their start on Katahdin, described a trail very different from the one we hike today. Here are just a few excerpts from their account:

> *As we approached Baxter Peak the fog which had been filling the Great Basin overflowed and spread out in swirling eddies over the entire mountain. This was a blessing in disguise, as it did away with the wish to linger on the summit, consuming time we could ill afford to spare. So, appearing to each other through the fog rather like moth-eaten ghosts, we picked our way along the first steps of the Appalachian Trail down to Hunt Spur.*

> *The next morning gave us our first example of what the trail might be expected to be like. For the most part the A.T. in Maine is a succession of old trails and wood roads joined together here and there by newly cut trail. The entire length is plainly marked every few rods with white titanium oxide paint blazes on trees.... The entire Trail is so well marked that only through carelessness would one stray away from it.*
>
> *At the end of each day's travel, the Trail leads to a comfortable sporting camp on some pond or lake. It is therefore unnecessary to carry food or bedding, and in case of bad weather one may put up as long as one wishes. These camps, designed to cater to hunters and fishermen from the cities, though rustic are very comfortable. It is usual to find them well situated, commanding an extensive view with a beautiful pond or lake in the foreground.... The food is usually excellent.*

Just imagine how popular the trail in Maine would be if, at the end of each day's hike, one could spend the evening on the deck of a rustic camp, enjoying the view out over a pond, lake or river, while digesting an excellent meal. It would be a different hiking experience, to be sure, but would also be one that appealed to the type of hiker Benton MacKaye had in mind when he first proposed the trail in 1921.

In Shenandoah National Park, early AT hikers could avail themselves of the hospitality of Skyland Lodge, conveniently located right next to the trail. When members of the Potomac Appalachian Trail Club began to build the trail through the territory that eventually became the park, they stayed overnight at Skyland, where they eagerly took part in the Lodge's nightly "frolics"—dances, music programs and amateur theater. Skyland is still there, of course, but operated these days by the National Park Service. And in the Peaks of Otter region near Lynchburg, the trail passed by the Hotel Mons, one of the beautiful resort hotels built in the Virginia mountains around the turn of the century. The Mons opened on the site of an earlier hotel in 1920 and was famous for the quality of its fried chicken and its pies. According to one source from the late 1930s:

> *To visit Hotel Mons was to develop "the Mons habit" and to several generations of Mons-goers the old hotel was a summer landmark. There they enjoyed the cool quiet of summer days in the beautiful Blue Ridge mountains. They enjoyed hearty meals supplied from country gardens and good companions for an evening stroll to mark the last colors of the sunset*

> *reflected against the two summits, Sharp Top and Flat Top—the Peaks of Otter. From Mons they returned home refreshed and replenished. And they returned to the mountain year after year.*

In addition to local residents with "the Mons habit," many an early Appalachian Trail hiker stayed at the Mons on his or her hikes north and south. The Mons did not survive the downturn in business during the Great Depression followed by the Second World War, and these days the trail passes well to the west of the Peaks of Otter, forcing hikers to stay at the much less scenic Bobblet's Gap Shelter. But from a point just north of the shelter they can gaze east to the Peaks of Otter and see where the Mons once stood and they can dream about fried chicken and hot fruit pies.

Grand hotels like the Mons dotted the early landscape of the Appalachian Trail, but by the 1950s, almost all of them were closed, done in by a combination of economic dislocation in the 1930s, a lack of visitors in the 1940s due to war-time restrictions or by the increasing ubiquity of the automobile, which made it possible for people visiting the mountains to go just about anywhere they wanted and not just to the larger, grander hotels from the turn of the century. Those mountain hotels, often located near thermal springs or in locations with pleasant vistas of the Appalachian Mountains, were increasingly replaced by small hotels catering to Americans with cars—soon to be known as "motels." If you want to see a relic of the high point of the American motel, take a drive through Front Royal, Virginia, just north of the north end of Shenandoah National Park. As you drive north and west through the city and approach the river, you'll pass half a dozen motels, all of which are still open but don't seem to cater to hikers quite as much as they once did. But in the 1950s and 1960s, people heading to the Appalachian Trail for a day hike could easily stay at one of the many motels along the trail's route, drive up into the park, have their hike and then either go back to the motel or head on home. Some of the old motels along the trail are still popular with long-distance hikers, but mostly they too have faded away, replaced by larger hotels like Holiday Inn or Days Inn clustered closer to interstates or at least major highways.

As the number of hikers along the trail grew in the 1960s and 1970s, a new kind of business began to appear along the Appalachian Trail to take up the slack from motels: the hiker hostel—a place to stay for the night set up specifically for hikers. These hostels sat somewhere between a motel and a private home in that they provided a wide variety of options depending on location. Some began by offering a dry place to sleep and a hot shower, others included the option to do laundry, some offered meals and some offered all of these amenities. The Church of the Mountain in the Delaware Water Gap region of Pennsylvania, which opened its doors to hikers in 1976, claims the status of being the first of the dedicated hiker hostels along the trail. But perhaps the most famous of the early hiker hostels was Woods Hole Hostel in Central Virginia. Opened to hikers in 1986 by Roy and Tillie Wood, Woods Hole has offered generations of hikers a place to spend the night, a hot shower, a great meal and, most importantly, Tillie's legendary peach cobbler. Located just south of Pearisburg, Virginia, Woods Hole was an old chestnut log house in the mountains that Roy and Tillie refurbished into first a weekend place for themselves and eventually a hostel for hikers. In many ways, Woods Hole became the model on which so many hiker hostels have been created. But it would be hard for any modern hostel to offer the same warmth and welcome that Roy and Tillie provided.

Over the decades, the proximity of the Appalachian Trail to so many towns and small rural communities has led to the rise in something today's hikers call "trail magic." Several years ago, my younger son and I were hiking on the trail in Maryland. We were out for three nights, and the weather was perfect. We're not a religious family, so it didn't dawn on either of us that it was Easter weekend, but that fact was brought home quickly to us in an unusual way just after we crossed a road on our way north. Someone had come onto the trail either early that morning or perhaps the night before and hung small plastic Easter eggs from tree branches along the trail. In each one, there was a Tootsie Roll and a small slip of paper with a Bible verse. We each took one, ate the candy and then stuffed the egg, verse and ribbon into our packs and carried it all out. Because we were on Day 2 of our hike, getting some free candy along the trail was the kind of freely given gift that just makes you smile. It's easy to look askance at the religious messages or the violations of Leave No Trace that those eggs represented, and the Leave No Trace enforcer in my soul was more than a bit unhappy about what amounted to littering on the trail. But I overcame my tendencies and left the other six or seven remaining eggs there for other hikers who might come along that day. In the parlance of the Appalachian Trail, what we experienced at that moment was "trail magic" brought to us that morning by a "trail angel."

Because trail angels and their magic are so common today from one end of the Appalachian Trail to the other, it might be tempting to think that trail

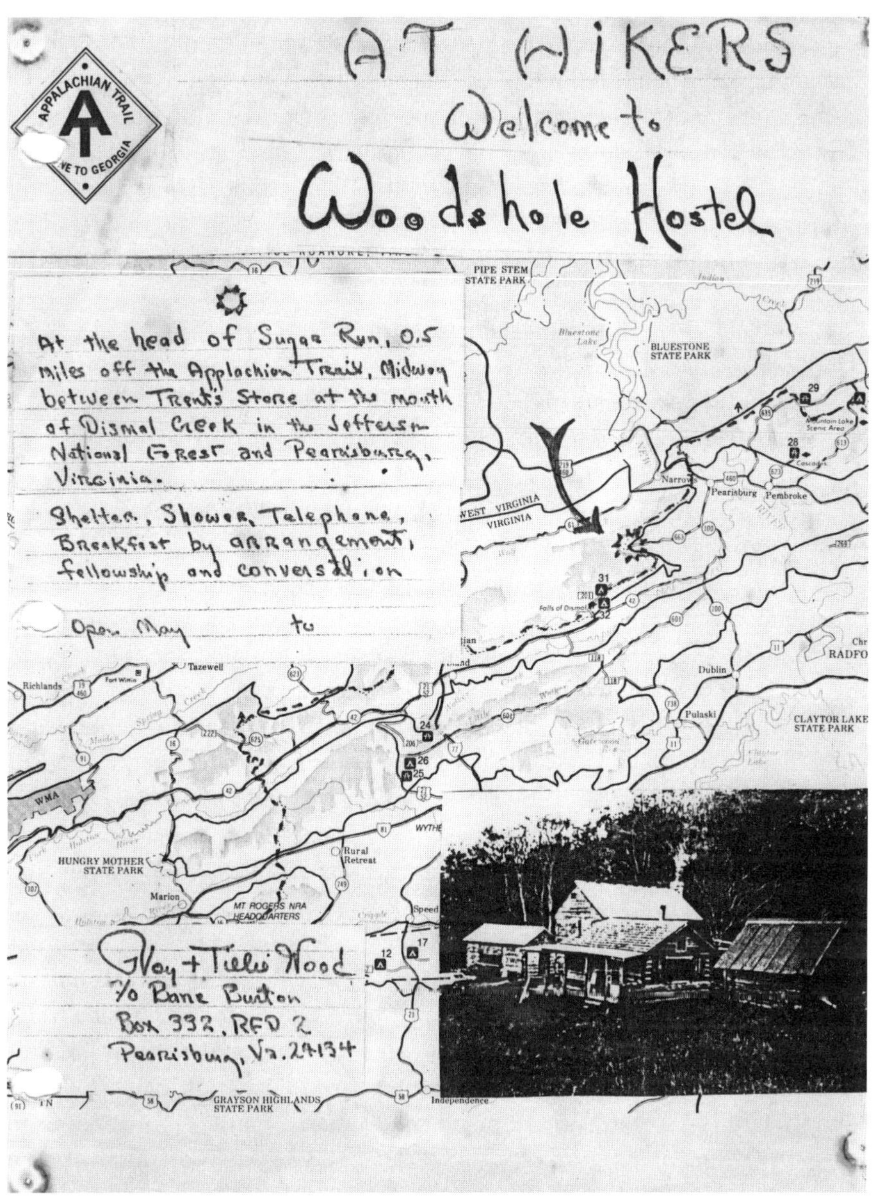

Flyer advertising Woods Hole Hostel, circa 1987. *Appalachian Trail Museum Archives.*

magic and trail angels are a post–World War II phenomenon—something that happened when the number of hikers on the AT began to grow rapidly in the 1960s. But trail magic and trail angels have been around since the start of the trail. To cite just one example of many that exist in the archives of the trail, in 1935 two young hikers ducked into a filling station along the trail in Virginia and spoke to the owner. They had been hiking in the rain for days and were more than a little bedraggled:

> *We told him our sad plight and were rewarded by an act of unbelievable kindness. The kind seldom encountered these days. He told us to go down to his house and make ourselves at home. He left us in the house alone, apparently trusting us completely.*

Trail magic can come in many forms. Many long-distance hikers are fond of saying things like "the trail provides," by which they mean the thing you need the most often shows up just when you need it the most. I've certainly experienced that. A few years ago, I was hiking a long section in Central Virginia in the summer heat. As I neared my destination for the night—the Punchbowl Shelter (the one said to be haunted by the ghost of Ottie Cline Powell)—I passed by a flowing spring and *should* have filled my water containers there. But I had to hike another two miles in the heat, most of it uphill, and so rather than carry the extra weight of all that water, I decided I'd just water up at the shelter where there is supposed to be a consistent spring. And there was. Sort of. The spring box just below the shelter had plenty of water in it, but it was about as disgusting as a water source can be. The surface was covered in an oily film, and there were two dead frogs floating in the yuck. I had two choices—dip water from the fetid little pond in front of the shelter and boil it or hike back almost two miles down the mountain to the spring I'd passed about an hour before. After a fair amount of waffling about what to do, I decided to leave my gear at the shelter and hike back to the spring with all my water containers. Just as I was about to leave the shelter, another hiker rolled in, headed down the mountain. When I explained my predicament, he happily gave me the rest of his water—enough to get me through the night and the morning—because he would hit the next spring north in under an hour. So yes, the trail does provide. Not always, but often enough for it to become something people talk about. And when it does, these days hikers call it just another example of trail magic.

Trail magic is a wonderful thing, but it's not uncontroversial and is not without its problems. As the number of hikers on the AT has grown over the past several decades, the number of people wanting to give back to the trail community has grown as well. Many of those folks very nicely decide they'll do some trail magic as a way of paying back kindnesses they experienced during their own hikes. Doing that is generous and much appreciated by hikers who benefit from whatever the trail angels provide. But many a well-intentioned trail angel has left food for hikers at a road crossing, a trailhead or at a shelter with the intention of returning the next day (or two) to retrieve their cooler or whatever else they packed the food in. Hikers arriving at the location where the food was left often find it scattered all over the ground by a bear, a raccoon or some other entrepreneurial animal. Finding piles of shredded food containers takes away from the hiking experience because it is now not trail magic and instead is just litter. More importantly, though, leaving food out for wild animals to find and consume makes those animals a bit less wild, encourages them to seek out and eat human food and habituates them to hanging around road crossings, trailheads and shelters.

The old saying "a fed bear is a dead bear" sticks around for a reason. Bears are very single-minded creatures that pretty much only think about eating (except during breeding season when they do get distracted from eating by other bears), and a cooler full of sandwiches is much tastier and more filling and easier to get at than a log full of ants and beetles. If they find a cooler of sandwiches somewhere, they almost certainly will return to that spot again and again seeking more of those tasty treats. And if humans are hanging around that spot—think asleep in or near a shelter—the fed bear is likely to start rooting around in the packs of those humans. Do that enough times and a bear is likely to be shot by park service or forest service personnel, and humans are likely to be a bit traumatized by having to fend off a hungry and very persistent bear that just wants another sandwich. The better version of this scenario is the one where the trail angel hangs around with their food, leaving none of it behind when they depart. The hikers who pass by are just as happy, and the bears that wander by later can only wonder what that interesting smell came from.

Trail magic in all its forms shines a light on one of the most important outgrowths of the creation of the Appalachian Trail. Over the decades, hikers and members of communities along the trail have come together to create something we now call the "trail community." The history of the AT is absolutely filled with examples of local residents providing kindnesses to hikers, everything from offering meals to rides to shelter to gear—just about anything one could imagine. Hikers didn't start calling it trail magic until sometime in the 1970s or 1980s, but it has always been a part of the history

Trail magic along the Appalachian Trail in North Carolina, 2024. *Photography by Stacia Bennett, used with permission.*

of the trail. Over the past fifty years, the number of hikers and backpackers using the Appalachian Trail has just grown and grown, and with that growth have come moments of significant anxiety about the future of the trail. As we saw earlier, that anxiety was focused on overuse of the trail shelters in the 1970s, and since 2010 or so, that anxiety has sometimes taken the form of a belief that too much trail magic was making the AT too easy to hike and was thus encouraging too many people to use the trail. The trail is certainly being overused in certain places that are either iconically beautiful or close to urban centers—think McAfee Knob in Virginia or Annapolis Rocks in Maryland. But these are exceptional cases. Except during peak leaf season, when tens of thousands of people hit the trail for views of the foliage, the Appalachian Trail remains a place where hikers can spend time in nature and see only a few other hikers during their day. In other words, "leaf magic" is much more responsible for any overcrowding on the trail than is "trail magic."

2,000-MILERS

It's a long trail…

—Chester Dziengielewski, writing in a trail register on Mount Oglethorpe, Georgia, after walking the entire Appalachian Trail southbound in 1951

So I trudge up and down mountain footpaths ever so tired. I long to see the beautiful sights before me. Outdoors is where I belong, with nature and God. The peaceful feeling of mountains gives me a high.

—Georgia, 1982

When the Appalachian Trail began, no one involved in the project imagined that a hiker would attempt to traverse the entire trail in one hiking season. Between 1925 and 1948, a small number of hikers completed the trail in sections—either Myron Avery or Eiler Larsen was the first man, and Mary Kilpatrick was the first woman to do so.

In the 1970s, a former Boy Scout from New York claimed that he and several of his friends hiked the entire trail in the 1930s, but his claims lacked any supporting evidence beyond his own assertions. It wasn't until 1948 that a World War II veteran and experienced backpacker named Earl Shaffer could prove that he did, indeed, hike from Georgia to Maine in the same hiking season, although when he completed his hike, Shaffer had to work hard to convince the ATC leadership that he actually managed it and that he wasn't trying to pull a fast one on them. Even after he convinced them that he truly did walk from Georgia to Maine, leaders at the ATC wrote in

George Outerbridge, Martin Kilpatrick (*holding sign*), an unknown hiker and Mary Kilpatrick on the trail in Pennsylvania in 1933. *Philadelphia Trail Club Archives.*

their newsletter that it was unlikely that anyone would accomplish the feat anytime soon because, as Jean Stephenson of the ATC put it,

> *Mr. Shaffer's immediate past experience had particularly conditioned him for a trip of this nature. It will probably be some time before anyone who attempts a through trip has the unusual experience and training that made it possible for Mr. Shaffer to succeed in such a journey.*

Stephenson was wrong, as it turns out, because in 1951 three men—Gene Espy, Chester Dziengielewski and Martin Papendick—hiked the whole two-thousand-plus miles of the trail, and one other, Bill Hall, hiked from Maine to Georgia but skipped a three-hundred-mile stretch so he could report to his draft board on time for service in the Korean War. The publicity surrounding the hikes of these men spurred others to make the attempt, and while the number of aspiring thru hikers remained small until the 1970s, that number did grow from year to year, eventually reaching flood stage in the early 2000s. In 2024, more than 2,000 hikers registered an attempt at a thru hike with the ATC, with something like half of them succeeding. When someone did complete a thru hike, the ATC made a big deal out of it. All successful thru hikers were invited to the ATC's annual dinner every year

Earl Shaffer after completing his thru hike in 1948. *Potomac Appalachian Trail Club Archives.*

and were given a handmade wooden plaque celebrating their achievement. But before they received their plaque, those hikers had to prove that they really had hiked the whole trail. Until 1972, the ATC had an "accreditation committee" that interviewed hikers claiming to be "2,000-milers," and the committee required a fair amount of documentation from them. But in 1974, the ATC threw in the towel. The previous year, almost 250 people had begun a thru hike, and the work of certifying their achievement now seemed overwhelming. Also, not everyone associated with the trail was happy with the ATC for making a big deal out of the thru hikers. In January 1974, ATC Chairman Stan Murray confessed to the person at ATC responsible for keeping track of the thru hikers:

> *You probably have received, as I have, criticism from an increasing number of sources on the emphasis we have been placing on 2,000-mile hikers. I have been giving this some thought and it is becoming more and more apparent that it is beginning to serve no practical value to keep detailed records and counts of those persons planning to hike and actually hiking the whole trail....I am wondering if it might not serve our purpose adequately if we simply recorded the names of those who claim to have hiked the Trail and recognize their achievement by a certificate.*

That is, indeed, what the ATC decided to do, and ever since, 2,000-milers have operated on an honor system. If someone writes to the ATC and claims a successful thru hike, the ATC sends them a certificate and a patch. But the Conservancy does maintain a list of everyone who claims to be a 2,000-miler, and it is available on its website.

The earliest thru hikers were a hardy bunch because they couldn't rely on a network of hiker hostels, stores catering to hikers or trail angels ready to drive them into town, give them a meal or provide water during periods of drought. They did sometimes experience those kindnesses and were able to stay in the homes of local residents who might take in boarders, but mostly they were on their own during their hikes. The early thru hikers also had to navigate a trail that was often in poor shape. But by the 1960s, trail maintenance had improved dramatically, and the trail was well marked and easy to follow, if not always easy to hike. From the 1960s to today, long-distance hikers on the Appalachian Trail often hit the trail at moments of transition in their lives. They may have just graduated from college; they may have recently retired, gotten divorced or become empty-nesters. They may want to reset their lives, lose weight or find out whether they have the inner strength to do something extremely difficult. They also want to do these things in the mountains, in nature, away from the pressures of daily life, in a place where they can see and hear wild things, inhale the way the forest smells after it rains, wake up with snow on their tent or reach a summit just in time to watch the sun dip below the horizon.

> *Prevent your hike from degenerating into a joyless march for miles. Let your purpose be this balance: to fully experience and appreciate this trail, <u>and</u> to prevail over all travails so as to arrive atop that final mountain.*
>
> —Philosopher's Guide, *1982*

A thru hike can be a life-changing experience. But it can also get boring. Hiking more than two thousand miles over several months becomes an exercise in repetition in which hikers do largely the same thing every day, walking through forests that look much the same from day to day, sleeping at or near shelters that vary only slightly, eating food that often varies less than the shelters. One of the ways thru hikers have avoided having their two-thousand-mile hike turn into a joyless death march is by creating a slew of traditions and challenges that help relieve the boredom of doing essentially the same thing every day—get up, pack up, hike fifteen miles, eat, go to sleep, repeat. Perhaps the most fun of all the hiker traditions is "Hike Naked Day." No one knows when Hike Naked Day began, but in his book about his 1970 thru hike, Ed Garvey reports meeting a group of unclothed hikers along the way. Hike Naked Day is unofficially on June 21 every year—the Summer Solstice—and on that day hikers willing to take the plunge are supposed to strip down and hike on. Given the prevalence of poison ivy, ticks and mosquitos (and fully clothed hikers) along the Appalachian Trail, not many actually do more than get naked and have a few photos taken, then get dressed again, but every year at least some fraction of the AT hiking public goes *au naturel* for at least part of the day.

> *It felt great hiking along, feeling the breeze, staying cool. The bugs seemed to stay away and the temperature was perfect. I came across a day hiker sitting in the woods. He looked up at me and simply said, "Oh, is it Hike Naked Day?"*
>
> —*New Hampshire, 2018*

Less frisky is the Half Gallon Challenge. When thru hikers reach the camp store in Pine Grove Furnace State Park, which is just a few miles north of the halfway point of the trail in Pennsylvania, if they are up for the challenge, they purchase a half gallon of ice cream and, sitting at one of the picnic tables outside, eat it all in one go. It seems that the manager of that camp store came up with the idea for the challenge in 1980, and ever since, some fraction of the thru hiking population has eaten, or at least attempted to eat, an entire half gallon of ice cream all at once. After they finish (or give up), they can stroll over to the nearby Appalachian Trail Museum while they digest all that butterfat. Another risk-free challenge is "confessing to the Priest" in the shelter register at the Priest Shelter in Virginia. Hikers confess to many things—stealing someone else's Pop-Tarts, not digging a cat hole when they poop in the woods or having lewd thoughts about other hikers. But the most common confessions seem to be about annoying other hikers in various ways.

> *Forgive me trail father or don't, for I have no shame. Sometimes I sing Christmas songs out loud despite the suffering it may cause my fellow hikers.*
>
> *—Priest Shelter, Virginia, 1988*

Perhaps the most difficult of the thru hiker challenges, though, is the "Four State Challenge." To accomplish this feat, northbound hikers begin at or near the Virginia/West Virginia line in Northern Virginia and hike through West Virginia and Maryland, finishing in Pennsylvania forty-five miles later. Southbounders hike into and through the same states, but in reverse order. Few hikers attempt this feat, and even fewer make all forty-five miles in twenty-four hours, but just knowing that the challenge is ahead of (or behind them) gives all hikers something new and different to think about and talk about as they keep marching north or south.

One of the more charming traditions of the Appalachian Trail is the determination of so many long-distance hikers to acquire and then devotedly use "trail names." If you meet a long-distance hiker on the Appalachian Trail these days, they are likely to introduce themselves by their trail name rather than the name that appears on their birth certificate or driver's license. Trail names can be descriptive (the Gambler, Sticks, Snappy, Apricot), or they can be an homage to a hiker's love of a fictional character. For decades, Tolkien-inspired names were very popular, and there have been many Frodos, Bilbos, Gandalfs, Goldberrys, Galadriels and Striders. Trail names often reference a moment in that hiker's experience (PigPen, Puff Puff), or they can be outright head scratchers like Pee Bottle or Jon Lite Shop. My own trail name is Grandaddy Spartan, which has the virtue of making everyone who hears it smile or chuckle. Almost all (but not all) thru hikers have a trail name; many long-distance hikers do as well, and some people who are more regular hikers have one too. There are many, many theories about how the use of trail names by hikers began and when, exactly, the practice started. Some people say that the first person to hike from Georgia to Maine in one year—Earl Shaffer—gets credit for dubbing himself "the Crazy One," but it seems he started using that term to describe himself years after his hike was over. Hikers certainly were beginning to use trail names by the early 1970s, but even at the end of the decade, trail names were much less common than they are today. The Appalachian Trail Museum maintains a database of thru hiker photographs taken at ATC Headquarters in Harpers Ferry that begins in 1979. In that first year, there are 162 photographs of hikers, but only 20 of those hikers used a trail name. Within a decade, though, almost all the hikers in the database used one. There are thousands and thousands of photographs in that archive, and a quick and dirty analysis of those names indicates that the most common choices in some way referenced bears—Yogi, Pooh, Grizzly and so on.

These days, the use of trail names is just one of the many traditions of the Appalachian Trail experience. But when they began, they provided hikers with a practical way to differentiate between different hikers named Paul or Cindy or Mike. Instead of, "Have you seen Mike this week?" or "Was Cindy at the shelter last night?" one could ask, "Have you seen Long Shanks this week?" or "Was Moonglow at the shelter last night?" and everyone who knew them by those names would know which Mike and which Cindy you were referring to. For solo hikers on the trail, using a trail name conferred (and still confers) a certain level of anonymity that they might want when sharing their names with people they don't know. That level of anonymity doesn't provide safety in the mountains, but at least it does keep a small amount of distance between hikers who might want to maintain that distance. Hikers didn't always want to be anonymous. Until the late 1960s, it was very common for short- or long-distance hikers to write their full name, mailing address and phone number in the shelter registers. In some cases, they explicitly wrote asking other hikers to get in touch, but even when they didn't, the implication was that hikers should feel free to do so. After all, why provide all your contact details if you *didn't* want people to contact you? Of course, there was no social media in those days, so the only way you *could* get in touch with other hikers was to leave them your coordinates in hopes they might reach out.

Tradition dictates that a trail name must be given rather than chosen, but not all hikers follow that tradition. For some who choose their own trail name, doing so is a kind of personal statement about who they are and how they see themselves in the world or the person they would like to be at some point. Trail naming can also point to the casual racism that has been a part of the history of the Appalachian Trail since its inception. When Krystal Williams, a Black woman, began her thru hike in 2011, a hiker tried to give her the trail name of "Brown Sugar." Krystal, an attorney and a very strong woman, simply said no thanks and chose the name "Bumble Bee" for herself—an homage to her favorite character in the Transformers movies and to prevent any further attempts to put an unintentionally racist, but still racist, name on her. For some hikers, their trail name, however they came by it, becomes part of their identity beyond the trail. They sign off on e-mails to friends as Dips or Two Steps or they use their trail name as a social media identifier.

When the trail first began, most hikers went into the mountains in groups, some of them quite large. But thru hikers were different. They came to the trail in pairs, perhaps groups of three or four, but mostly alone. They made friends along the way, but those friendships were ephemeral—two hikers might meet at a shelter, hike together for a few days or even a few weeks and then part company. They might reconnect somewhere up the trail, but most often they didn't. But sometime in the past few of decades, thru hikers began to form a trail family—"a tramily"—that they often stayed in for most or even all of their hike. In this way, they unintentionally re-created the form of group hiking that was so prevalent on the trail until at least the 1960s. The feelings of friendship and shared struggle found in trail families, or just with other hikers they meet along the way, are often very strong, so strong that hiking alone can become difficult to bear. In the summer of 2016, I found the following entry in the shelter register at the Thunder Ridge Shelter in Virginia:

> *This will be my second night in a row with a shelter to myself unless someone rolls in late. After taking my planned 4 day stop at home with my family, I have lost all the other Northbounders. I've been feeling increasingly homesick today, until the point where I was crying, eating my dinner, while being eaten alive by a swarm of bugs and then plotting all of the places I could get off the trail early. But that's not what I really want. After 2 days at home I'd be bored and wishing I was back out here. I love the AT, I'm just lonely. So here is my compromise: If I don't meet up with any other*

> *north bounders in the next day and half, I will shuttle forward to catch up with some other hikers. I don't like it, but it's better than hiking without enjoying the hike or stopping early.*

In addition to those hikers who attempt to hike the entire trail in one year, there is a second group of 2,000-milers—those who hike the length of the trail in sections over multiple years. Some of those hikers spread their hike out over just a few years, while others may take decades to complete the entire trail. Section hiking more easily fits into busy lives because a hiker can take a week here, a month there or just a long weekend to knock off one section or another. I'm one of those dogged section hikers but have only managed to hike a little over six hundred miles of the trail. In some ways, though, it's logistically and physically a little easier to hike it all in one year. For one thing, thru hikers don't have to arrange rides back and forth to the trail as they attempt to complete yet another section. Section hikers also never really develop "trail legs," the kind of leg strength and endurance that thru hikers find in themselves after weeks or months of hiking up and down mountains. Just when a section hiker is starting to feel really fit, it's time to go home. Section hikers also have to face the regular questioning of friends, "Have you finished the whole trail yet?" But section hikers don't have to have all the funds necessary for a thru hike all at once, they don't have to figure out how to take four or five months off from their lives, they don't have to have the emotional fortitude that it takes to keep going month after month and they know that before long they'll be home in their own beds after a hot shower and a good meal.

Regardless of their reason for attempting to hike the entire Appalachian Trail in one season, all thru hikers are, to one degree or another, on a classic hero quest. They launch themselves into the wild with only the gear on their backs and the clothes they are wearing, hoping to hike more than two thousand miles over several months. Some of them leave their starting point with a specific personal goal, some sort of transformation they hope their hike will bring to their lives. Others just start walking with no goal beyond reaching the other end of the trail. But each of them is changed by the experience in ways both mundane and profound. As 2021 thru hiker Sarah Robison ("Serendipity") put it recently:

> *At 11:20am on Monday, October 11, after 207 days of life on foot I summited the majestic 5269 feet of Mama K., Mount Katahdin. Not only does the wooden sign that rests atop her peak signify the northern terminus*

of the Appalachian Trail, but my arrival to its legs signified my evolution of self, my confidence, my courage, my strength, my fearlessness, my acceptance, my patience, my wanderlust. My willingness, my dedication, my grit, my pain, my faith, my trust, I did the thing. I did the thing, which was to let go.

TRAIL CLUBS

As far as possible the blazing and constructing of the trail and building of camps should be done by volunteer workers. For volunteer "work" is really "play."

—Benton MacKaye, 1921

The Appalachian Trail would not exist without the more than thirty volunteer trail clubs whose members provide tens of thousands of hours each year to help keep the trail open, clear of obstruction and as free of encroaching briars and nettles as possible. They built and now maintain the more than 250 shelters and privies. They pick up trash left behind by thoughtless hikers. They offer directions and advice to hikers who need it and friendship and support to those who want it. They promote the trail to new audiences and fight invasive species. They watch out for poachers—animal, wildflower and tree—and collaborate with local law enforcement when there is a problem on the trail. They join search-and-rescue operations when a hiker goes missing. They replace registers in the shelters when they fill up, and they keep springs as clear of obstruction as possible. They install erosion devices—water bars, check dams—and build bridges, lateral drains, walkways and other things that help hikers keep their feet dry. They do their best to keep hikers from cutting switchbacks (which makes erosion worse), and when the trail needs to be relocated, it is trail club volunteers who do the heavy work of making that happen. They run educational programs at trailheads and take groups of children on nature

Members of the Potomac Appalachian Trail Club on the trail in the 1930s. *Potomac Appalachian Trail Club Archives.*

hikes. They answer countless questions from hikers who reach out to their offices and produce detailed maps of whatever section of trail they are responsible for. They make, put up and replace signs all along the trail so hikers know where they are going, and each year they repaint the white blazes on the trees, rocks and fence posts that help hikers know they are still on the AT. In short, local trail club volunteers do the hundreds of things—big and small—that make the Appalachian Trail the wonderful hiking experience it is for millions of people every year.

In the early days of the Appalachian Trail, a very large number of the people who hiked on the trail were club members or their friends—often hitting the trail in large groups, sometimes very large groups. Those group hikes were important parts of the social lives of the trail club members, and many of the clubs that take care of the trail have continued this tradition of weekly and sometimes more than weekly hikes throughout the year. Those hikes were also important for growing the membership in the clubs as a way of luring in potential volunteers—go for a hike, have fun and then join us for some heavy work on the trail. Of course, club members were strongly encouraged to help build and maintain the trail, but it was always a minority of trail club members who did the dirty work of building the trail and then keeping it open. Right from the start, women played prominent roles in the clubs and often were the majority of the membership in a given club. A few of the clubs even imposed 50/50 rules because they had so many female members and wanted to try to keep a balanced membership. According to trail historian Sarah Mittlefehldt:

> *For many women from, especially, the upper classes, it was an opportunity for them to step out a little bit of traditional gender roles, but it was still socially acceptable for them to be part of these clubs. The clubs served a social club function but also had opportunities for them to literally get out of the home and house and become more engaged in the community in different ways.*

As the Appalachian Trail has become a more popular destination for hikers, fewer and fewer of those hikers are connected to the trail clubs in any way. They have, as Silas Chamberlin put it, become consumers of the trail rather than contributors to the trail. Over the decades since the 1970s, trail club volunteers have received their fair share of praise, and sometimes criticism, from hikers they meet out in the mountains or in the registers left at shelters. Most of the complaining has been about the state of this or that section of the trail—why hasn't the poison ivy been cut back from the footpath, where are the blazes marking the turn to the shelter—but mostly hikers have been very appreciative of the efforts of the trail clubs.

> *The trail from here to Moosilauke was very enjoyable and quite well-maintained. Good job Dartmouth Outing Club!*
>
> —*New Hampshire, 1991*

The clubs have always relied on local area residents and students to volunteer to keep the trail shipshape. Local residents have been especially important to the trail over the years because they are much more connected to nearby communities and were often very invested in the environment of their local mountains. Some who joined a club hike were lured into becoming volunteers after their experiences on the trail and after learning about the work of trail club volunteers. But as the Appalachian Trail becomes more of a national and even international phenomenon, those who hiked and now

Shelter maintainers Tawnya and Curt Finney at the Tumbling Run Shelters in Pennsylvania, 2020. *Photograph by Sarah Jones Decker, used with permission.*

hike on the trail come from everywhere and have much less connection to the local environment, are highly unlikely to join a trail club because the clubs are so far away and may never return to the AT after their one hike on it—whether it is for a few days or for a few months. In other words, they lack the connection to the trail that so many hikers had in the trail's first half-century.

The trail clubs have also been central to finding the best route for the trail through the Appalachian Mountains. One of the truisms about the AT is that the trail's route is constantly changing. When Myron Avery declared the trail complete in 1937, it was 2,050 miles long. This year, it is over 2,197 miles and follows a route substantially different in some sections than the one hikers would have followed in earlier decades. For example, in 1952, the ATC decided to abandon around 300 miles of the trail in Southwest Virginia at the urging the leadership of the Roanoke Appalachian Trail Club. The original route took hikers along Iron Mountain north of the Grayson Highlands (where the trail is today) and then across the New River near Galax on a pole ferry, and on east through the Dan River Gorge. The new route between Damascus and Dragon's Tooth that opened in 1953 is essentially the one hikers follow today. Similarly, at the urging of the Georgia

Appalachian Trail Club, the ATC abandoned a little over 35 miles of the trail at its southern terminus in the late 1950s. In those days, the AT began (or ended) on Mount Oglethorpe, but hikers leaving the mountaintop had to pass through some very smelly chicken farms on their way to Springer Mountain (the current southern terminus). Not surprisingly, giving up the chicken farm section of the trail was an easy decision.

Perhaps the best-known rerouting of the trail happened in the 1980s in Northern Virginia. After the passage of the National Trails System Act in 1968, landowners on Mount Weather canceled their easements for the trail, forcing hikers to walk for more than fifteen miles on a paved road. In the 1980s, a team from the Potomac Appalachian Trail Club found a new route that ran along the shoulders of the mountain, and the infamous "Roller Coaster" was born. Trail club members also helped with the land acquisition process after the AT became a national park. Rather than have federal personnel approach local landowners, the park service and the ATC decided instead to have local club members make the initial approach. The idea was that landowners would be much more open to a discussion about the sale of their land if they were chatting with someone from their community rather than from Washington. That strategy paid off, as most (but certainly not all) of the land acquisition process went forward without contention.

Some of the trail clubs are large and well financed, while others can be very small and have almost no funds to work with. The list of clubs maintaining the trail today is somewhat different than it was in the 1930s—some clubs have stopped working on the trail and others have joined the project. But all the clubs still share Benton MacKaye's original vision for the trail—that it would be built by and maintained by volunteers. This arrangement is unique among the national parks because while all the parks depend on volunteers to help with many aspects of park administration, nowhere else is a park maintained essentially entirely by volunteer clubs. The relationship between the National Park Service, the ATC and the thirty volunteer clubs requires constant care, but it has worked reasonably well since the AT became a national park in 1968. Hikers of all types are the ultimate beneficiaries of this unusual arrangement.

HIKING WHILE OTHER

As I was walking into Harpers Ferry, it just really struck me that I was, in the bright light of day, walking through woods that people who look like me and maybe even some of my ancestors and relatives had to traverse that same terrain in the dead of night to escape the horrific conditions of slavery. And I just broke out into tears. It was this weird combination of the weight of history and the profound freedom of the privilege I was experiencing in that moment.

—Krystal Williams ("Bumble Bee"), 2011

As wonderful as the Appalachian Trail is and as welcoming as it can be to anyone who wants to spend a few hours, a few days or a few months walking from white blaze to white blaze, not everyone has felt welcome along the trail. Not every hiker has been encouraged to walk on the trail, and not every hiker feels comfortable there today—and their discomfort has a history.

When the Appalachian Trail began in 1925, it passed through four states—Virginia, North Carolina, Tennessee and Georgia—that were formally segregated and through many others where hikers of color would have, and sadly still have, unpleasant experiences in towns or along roads. Until recently, Black Americans and other people of color would have found hiking in the mountains a risky or even dangerous endeavor, so there is no evidence that they took those risks in any great number until at least the 1970s. In some cases, it was impossible for a non-White person to join a trail club. For example, at its founding, the Smoky Mountains Hiking Club formally barred anyone who wasn't White from membership. Many of the other clubs used less obvious stratagems to make sure Black people, Jews and others were excluded from their ranks. Until at least the 1970s, one could not just sign up and join most of the trail clubs. Instead, potential new members had to pass an eye test. Nomination by two members was generally required, and the candidate for membership often had to take part in two or more club activities—a hike, a day of trail work and so on—before they could be admitted into the membership. In this way, existing club members could ensure that candidates for membership were "the right sort." The ATC was no better. For many decades, the Conference held annual meetings for its members that alternated between Southern locations and Northern ones. Those Southern meetings of the Conference were held in segregated lodgings or in venues where a person of color would feel highly unwelcome. Even if a hiker of color wanted to attend one of the Conference's annual meetings in the South, they couldn't or would be doing so at great personal risk.

I've spent most of the past decade looking for examples of non-White hikers along the Appalachian Trail or evidence that the ATC and the trail clubs actively tried to change the demographic imbalance in the hiking population. Until the turn of the most recent century, there is very little evidence of any such effort and only scant evidence of diversity in the hiker population. It's important to note here that we know next to nothing about the race or ethnic background of casual hikers who went and now go onto the AT for a few hours or a few days. But we do know *something*. What we know is that it is extremely difficult to find *any* evidence of non-White hikers on the AT until after 1990 or so, and what evidence one can find is pretty scarce. For example, of the almost 170 hiker photos from 1979 in the AT hiker picture database maintained by the AT Museum, only one of those hikers appears to be Black. The first instance of a photograph of a Black hiker in the *Appalachian Trailway News* (the ATC's newsletter) that I've found is from the 1980s, and then there isn't another such photograph until the late 1990s. Hikers of color were certainly out on the AT after 1970, but they are just very hard to find. And for good reason. Hikers of color likely knew better than to call attention to their presence. This photograph taken at the AMC's Galehead Hut sometime in the 1980s is one of the few I've been able to locate with hikers of color before the 1990s.

Even if hikers of color worked up their nerve to get out on the trail, the AT could be and still can be a very unfriendly and even threatening place

A group of young hikers at the Galehead Hut, New Hampshire, circa 1980s. *Appalachian Mountain Club Archives.*

for those who aren't White. For example, in the 1981 shelter register from the Montray (now Tray Mountain) Shelter in Georgia, someone wrote, "All Niggers Will Die Here!" across the top of one of the pages in the register. That kind of threat is disturbing enough, but what makes it worse is that not one hiker who followed the person who wrote that threat saw fit to scratch it out or tear it out, leaving it there in the register for everyone else to find when they reached the shelter. It's not difficult to imagine what it might have felt like to have been a Black hiker who, after toiling up the trail for a day, found that in the shelter register. Hikers who were not heterosexual also faced discrimination and abuse on the trail, and the shelter registers contain more than their fair share of anti-LGBTQ slurs and threats. In 1998, Robert Taylor became the first Black man to thru hike the Appalachian Trail (and subsequently the Pacific Crest Trail). In the one interview he gave about his hike, in *Backpacker Magazine*, Taylor reported that most of the racism he experienced came from the residents of small towns along the trail, but sometimes fellow hikers could send subtle or not-so-subtle signals about their attitudes toward a Black hiker:

> *My problems were mainly with people. In towns, people yelled racist threats at me in just about every state I went through. They'd say, "We don't like you," and "You're a nigger." Once when I stopped at a mail drop, the postmaster said, "Boy, get out of here. We got no mail drop for you." Even on the trail itself, other AT thru-hikers acted like I was going to steal their gear. I remember thinking, "I'm not going to steal any of your stuff. I'm having a hard enough time carrying mine."*

Hikers, whether they were people of color or not, noticed that the trail passed close to a number of "sundown towns," towns where non-White people needed to be off the streets by sundown. Perhaps the most infamous of those was Erwin, Tennessee, a town where one of America's most horrible lynchings took place in 1918. Following the lynching of Thomas Devert, the entire Black population of Erwin was expelled from town and told to never return. As late as the 1980s, hikers on the AT were aware of this history. As one hiker wrote in the nearby Curly Maple Shelter's register in 1988, "What is it about a town that prides itself on having no black residents?" It wasn't just hikers of color who found the Appalachian Trail to be an unwelcoming place. As recently as 2018, I was asked by a Black shuttle driver if I could meet him on the edge of the popular trail town of Duncannon, Pennsylvania, so he could drive me back to my car forty miles to the south. When I asked him why he wanted me to walk to the edge of town, he told me he was tired of people in that officially designated "A.T. Community" yelling at him and sometimes even throwing things at his van.

It can be challenging to find evidence of the presence of Black Americans anywhere along the Appalachian Trail, with two exceptions: the Brown

Mountain Creek community in Central Virginia and the Cesar Brook campsite in Connecticut. As hikers head north or south near Lynchburg, they will find a few interpretive signs along the trail, put there by a U.S. Forest Service ranger more than two decades ago, that commemorate the presence of the Black community that lived along Brown Mountain Creek for three generations after being freed from enslavement in 1865. The trail parallels the creek, and all along that section, you can see the labor of those generations—stone walls built to control the flow of the stream, the foundations of homes and an old gristmill and flat spaces where the community grew corn and flax. In Connecticut, the Ceser Brook campsite is popular with hikers. Until 2022, those hikers would have been forgiven for not knowing that it was once the land of the Cesar family, a family of free Blacks who celebrated both the Fourth of July and the passage of the Fifteenth Amendment (guaranteeing the right to vote regardless of race) on the summit of the mountain. The broadside they put out in 1870 about the celebration invited all their neighbors to come join in the festivities, assuring some that "White spectators of respectability, will be treated well." If it weren't for the efforts of a group of students at the nearby Salisbury School in 2021 who discovered the story of the Cesar family as part of a class project, the signage at the campsite still would have made no reference to the family and would have continued to misspell their name.

The Appalachian Trail community has, until very recently, also done a very good job of ignoring the presence of Indigenous people along the trail's route through what the original residents of the Appalachian Mountains call Turtle Island. Other than a few mentions in the old trail guides, one would be hard-pressed to find any recognition in the publicity for the trail or in histories of the trail that the Indigenous presence in the Appalachian Mountains stretches back thousands and thousands of years. It's all but impossible to find any recognition of the genocide of Native peoples who lived in the mountains of the East. Indigenous knowledge about living in harmony with nature, about the effective management of mountain ecosystems or the many dozens of ways that Indigenous people situate themselves in the world through stories rooted in physical places—all these things are essentially absent from the history of the AT. According to Professor Trey Adcock, a member of the Cherokee Nation and a professor at UNC–Asheville, the Appalachian Trail passes through the traditional lands of twenty-two Native nations. But the vast majority of hikers couldn't name more than two or three of those nations. The virtual absence of the Indigenous presence from the stories hikers learn and later tell about their experiences on the trail is just one of the many ways the Appalachian Trail was a bastion of whiteness for most of its history.

But change is happening. In the past few decades, the ATC, the National Park Service and the trail clubs have begun to try to address the many ways hikers who aren't White access the trail, feel welcomed on the trail and are acknowledged as part of the trail's history. Whether the park service will continue to do so in the coming years is certainly an open question as we enter the trail's second century. There is still plenty of work to do if the Appalachian Trail is to achieve Benton MacKaye's vision as a place where "people," not just one kind of people, can go into the mountains for a few hours, a few days or for a longer stretch to find solutions to "the problem of living."

FOREST BATHING

Well, it's been rainy, foggish, and cloudesque all day today. However, I have found that there are, even in the most unpromising of weather, sights to be seen. The rolling fog out over the East and West Carrie Ponds gave it an unparalleled glowing effect. The rain in the mossy forests brings out the colors, and although there is no far-reaching view from any point, the clouds isolate high areas giving one an incredibly unearthly feeling.

—*Maine, 1983*

On an early page of this book, I offered a poem to start our story of the trail's history. That poem was written just for me at a "pop-up poetry" event in Banff, Alberta, in November 2023 by Richard Harrison. If you've never been to a pop-up poetry event, you really must try to attend one because they can be magical experiences. Poetry, like backpacking, is *hard*. At a pop-up event, poets sit at manual typewriters and ask attendees what they would like a poem about. When Richard asked me what I wanted, I told him that I was a backpacker and wanted a poem about what it was like to leave civilization behind and go into the mountains for a few days and just be. He thought about it for a minute, smiled and said, "I have something, and if it's too short, say so and I'll write something longer for you." When I saw what he'd written, I told him no, it's perfect, because it explains the specific aspect of human existence that I was hoping his poem would address. As hikers, we try to take the fewest possible steps to get from one place to another, and Richard's poem did just that, but with the fewest possible words.

The Unaka Mountains and Lake Santeetlah, circa 1930. *Photograph by George Masa, Appalachian Trail Conservancy Archives.*

Forest bathing (*Shinrin-yoku*) is a relatively recent practice in Japan, based on three very traditional ideas—*yūgen*, *komorebi* and *wabi-sabi*. *Yūgen* is what happens when you are so deeply aware of the beauty of the world around you that the emotions that beauty calls into being can't be expressed in words—you just have to feel them. *Komorebi*, which translates as sunlight leaking through trees, signifies the beauty that one sees in the interplay of light as it dapples the forest floor, suddenly highlighting a cluster of wildflowers or leaving cool dark spaces in its wake. *Wabi-sabi* is the traditional Buddhist celebration of impermanence and imperfection—something one sees that signifies the impermanence of all things has an inherent beauty. Think of the last leaves of autumn clinging to a branch, hinting at the riot of color that spread across the mountain just weeks before but now has faded to brown. Those leaves will fall, leaving bare limbs behind, and will rot away on the ground, nourishing the forest for another year, another cycle of growth, beauty and decay. Appreciating the beauty of those last few leaves is just one example of *wabi-sabi*. Together, these three ways of perceiving the natural world sum up the idea of forest bathing.

The Appalachian Trail in the fog, 2022. *Photograph by the author.*

Since the beginning of the Appalachian Trail, many hikers have been engaged in forest bathing, even though they wouldn't have used that term to describe their experiences. Only recently have psychologists and cognitive scientists begun to recognize the therapeutic benefits of this practice, but Appalachian Trail hikers have known those benefits for one hundred years. Sometimes they struggle to put their feelings into words, but over the decades they *have* managed to write down just what they were feeling in the shelter registers. One of the things that jumps off the pages of those registers is the profound sense of wonder and pleasure that hikers derive from being in the mountains, from being in nature. They really do experience both *yūgen* and *komorebi*:

> *The light shot through a leafy screen sprinkled with water drops. Wild birds presented their hypnotic symphony. Rocks aren't obstacles, instead they are*

> *natural statues of past motion and force. These sights of wilderness I have seen, which others have seen as monsters and remarks on nature's weakness. Take heart, a man is part of wildness and observer at the same time.*
>
> —*Vermont, 1973*

> *The rain was beautiful last night—mesmerizing—and I stayed up real late after it had stopped just watching the fire crackle. Wow, this life stuff is pretty good; there's plenty of it in these woods, too.*
>
> —*Maine, 1983*

But there is more to what hikers experience in the mountains than just seeing those beautiful flowers, the dying of the light over the ridgetop at sunset, hearing the faraway call of a loon on a Maine pond or seeing their first bear ambling down the trail ahead of them. Being in the mountains alters our perceptions of the volume of space surrounding us. The great environmental writer Barry Lopez urged his readers to pay close attention to those changes in perception:

> *Where in this volume of space are you situated? The space behind you is as important as what you see before you. What lies beneath you is as relevant as what stands on the far horizon. Actively use your ears to imagine the acoustical hemisphere you occupy. How does birdsong ramify here? Through what kind of air is it moving? Concentrate on smells in the belief you can smell water and stone. Use your hands to get the heft and texture of a place—the tensile strength in a willow branch, the moisture in a pinch of soil, the different nap of leaves.*

Writers like Lopez have long understood how the experience of nature changes the way we experience the spaces we occupy. The world around us can seem so much larger and our connection to it so much greater when we are in the wild—we have a true sense of being present in the world, a much larger world than we possibly can in the confines of urban environments.

> *The greenness of the mountains is intense on these misty days & the glow of the flowers is astounding. I'm so glad to be back in the mountains. The hike ahead will be difficult, but no matter, with beauty surrounding it can never get too difficult.*
>
> —*Georgia, 1981*

Not that long ago, I was on top of a mountain in the Southern Appalachians, just taking a wandering walk before bed. I had hiked ten or twelve miles that day, my campsite was all set up, my dinner was consumed and cleaned up and my bear bag was already hanging from a branch. I could have declared it to be "hiker midnight" (bedtime, regardless of the time of day), but because it was late June, the days were very long, the weather was warm but not hot and there was a feeling of tension in the air that I just wanted to explore. I wandered up toward the summit, which was bare of trees but covered in low-growing, dense bushes that made it difficult to see more than a few feet off the trail but which allowed me to see the entire mountaintop if I raised my gaze. I could hear birds and some sort of smallish mammal in the bushes, and it was nice to just be aware of their presence. Less nice was when I heard the cry of a bear cub off to my right. He or she seemed to be calling out for their mother, and I definitely did not want to meet her on this confined section of trail, so I moved farther up to the summit. It was there that I could see not only the mountain I was on but also the ones off to the east and the west of me. And I could see dark clouds blowing in from the northwest, which explained the tension I was feeling in the air around me. As I stood there watching the clouds scud my way, the space I was standing in became both larger and smaller at the same time. There were mountains all around me, but the rising levels of ozone in the air meant that the coming storm was beginning to press on me like a physical weight. I knew I needed to get off the summit because summits are bad places to be when a summer thunderstorm arrives, but I also wanted to feel the rising power of the storm as it began to rumble and flash.

If you've been on top of a mountain when a thunderstorm rolls in, you know that feeling—the sense that the hard cobalt sky is pressing itself down and into you, the feeling of expectation, almost like the forest is holding its breath, the sudden quiet of the birds and the upsurging songs of frogs and insects. If I'd been smarter, I would have left the mountain and run for my tent—mother bear be damned—but I wasn't smarter. I wanted to *feel* that storm as it arrived—not the lightning, of course, but the raw energy of a mountain storm all around me. Fortunately for me, it never broke over the summit I was on. Instead, I was able to watch it fly away to the east, throwing bolt after bolt of lightning onto distant ridges. Standing there alone on top of the mountain was stupid but exhilarating at the same time. I was briefly a part of the storm without being a part of it. I was intensely aware of my own humanity and my own fragility and, most importantly, of my place on the earth at that moment. I could feel the mountain under me, solid, ancient, even as the winds whipped around me and the thunder vibrated all the way into my bones. I didn't want to be hit by lightning. I didn't want to die. But I wanted to be part of the elemental symphony filling my ears, touching my skin, making the hair on my arms and neck stand up. I wanted to live in that storm. And I wanted to wake up the next morning, snug in my sleeping bag, when it was all over.

> *It's amazing how beautiful the skies are at night in the mountains. Nothing like the city back home! After those rains yesterday it sure was nice waking up to the sun and clear skies above. Oh it's beautiful!*
>
> —*Virginia, 1984*

CONCLUSION

Walking creates trails. Trails in turn, shape landscapes. And, over time, landscapes come to serve as archives of communal knowledge and symbolic meaning.

—Robert Moor, On Trails, *2016*

When I stood I thought I glimpsed my own desire. The landscape and the animals were like something found at the edge of a dream.

—Barry Lopez, Arctic Dreams, *1986*

Seen from the perspective of hikers, in many ways, the history of the Appalachian Trail is a history of three different versions of the trail that overlap one another. The original version, which hikers could first walk on in the mid-1920s, was little more than a hope, an idea that would one day become an iconic path through the mountains imitated by many but never quite equaled by those that have come along since. While well designed and well blazed, that early version of the trail relied heavily on roads, whether paved, gravel or old abandoned wagon roads in the mountains. Because the trail-building clubs just wanted to get the thing done, they used whatever they had available to them, and mostly what they had available was roads. What that meant for hikers was that the Appalachian Trail they walked on was often not what we think of today as a trail but rather was a way to get from one ridge top to another.

Eiler Larsen on the Appalachian Trail in New Hampshire, 1930. *Appalachian Trail Conservancy Archives.*

Despite the road walking, the first version of the Appalachian Trail was beautiful and offered hikers a true wilderness experience. In many sections, they really could get away from civilization and walk through forests of mature trees, skirt boulder fields on mountaintops and drop deep into forested glens that were sometimes so dark that they felt almost primeval. They could trudge through the fogs and winds of the White Mountains and stumble along over tree roots and protruding stones in Vermont. They crossed rivers by wading or by paying a nickel to be put across in a leaky flat-bottomed boat, or they paddled themselves in canoes left for their use. But they also walked on roads much more than they might have preferred, they stayed in private homes or at fishing camps, they put up in hotels and motels along those highways and they listened to cars and trucks roaring by on nearby roads and scenic drives. That first version of the trail might have been well blazed, but it often suffered from a lack of maintenance, especially during the Second World War, when it received almost no care at all; by 1946, it was substantially grown over and clogged with blowdowns and the detritus of landslides and sometimes logged off in ways that made those blazes impossible to find.

Most of the hikers one might meet on the AT between 1925 and 1960 or so were there for the day or for a weekend. To be sure, some hikers—like George W. Outerbridge and his friends the Kilpatricks, troops of Boy or Girl Scouts, trail club outings, scattered church groups and the like—were out there for a week or even a few weeks at a time. And a few hardy souls were trying to hike it all, starting with Eiler Larsen, who managed the feat in sections between 1930 and 1936, and then Earl Shaffer, who hiked from Georgia to Maine in 1948; Gene Espy; Chester Dzingeliewski; and Martin Papendick, who managed the same feat in 1951; Mildred Norman and Richard Lamb, in 1952, who were the first flip-floppers to complete the trail in one year; and a few others like Grandma Gatewood and Dorothy Laker over the coming decade. But in the end, almost all the hikers on

Hikers at the Rattle River Trailhead, New Hampshire, circa 1970s. *Appalachian Mountain Club Archives.*

the Appalachian Trail until the late 1960s were not trying to accomplish something big, something momentous like a thru hike. They weren't trying to remake their own lives or prove that they weren't dead yet. They were there for the simpler joys of walking in the mountains, seeing their first bear, cooking a meal over an open fire at a shelter and for the fellowship of friends whom they hit the trail with.

Sometime in the 1960s, a new group of AT hikers began to emerge—the hikers who *did* want to accomplish something big, to prove something to themselves or to others, who wanted to conquer the trail or at least long sections of it. Their reasons were as many and varied as the hikers themselves, but those longer-distance hikers helped bring into being the second version of the trail, one that lay on top of the original version but could easily be missed unless you happened to be at a shelter when one or a group of those longer distance hikers showed up. Those hikers increasingly went by brow-furrowing trail names, they hiked faster and farther each day than the casual hikers could imagine, they had their own vocabulary, they subsisted on foods that more casual hikers found puzzling and even disgusting and they smelled pretty bad. There was just a funk surrounding them, a kind of miasma of sweat, dirt, soggy clothing, tobacco or cannabis smoke and possibly stale beer.

> *This is my first time on the AT. I hope to come back and do the whole thing one summer. (Of course, this is the first day and I don't smell yet!)*
>
> —*Tennessee, 1991*

But they smiled, they laughed, they teased one another and they filled the registers not so much with prosaic meditations on the beauty of the mountains, but instead with news of one another, with advice on where the best all-you-can-eat buffets were, complaints about trail conditions and compliments for the trail maintainers. Those hikers also began to create their own traditions—Hike Naked Day, the Half Gallon Challenge, the Four State Challenge and so on. As their numbers grew, a discernable "bubble" of long-distance and (at least intended) thru hikers appeared with some regularity along the trail, spawning businesses—gear stores, hiker hostels—that catered to their needs, or at the least causing stores along the trail to stock up on peanut butter, Slim Jims, Pop-Tarts and other hiker necessities during whatever time of year those longer-distance hikers could be expected in town. Local post offices prepared for their bounce boxes, and trail clubs increasingly monitored what was happening at the shelters they were

Hikers at the Garfield Ridge Shelter, New Hampshire, 1971. *Appalachian Mountain Club Archives.*

responsible for to make sure the hikers had what they needed and behaved in the ways they should.

The appearance of growing numbers of longer-distance hikers coincided with a more general expansion in the hiking public. More and more Americans—and visitors to America—turned to the mountains to find peace in a chaotic world, to test their fitness, to get back to nature and to just have a fun day under the trees. Whether they were out for just the afternoon, a few days or for months, the Appalachian Trail those hikers walked on was one in transition. The passage of the National Trails System Act first resulted in many landowners canceling easements and kicking the trail off their land, which generally meant even more road walking in the early 1970s. At the same time, with the trail now a national park, the National Park Service, working closely with the local trail clubs, began routing more and more of the trail into wilder locations. When a new section opened, hikers could count on it being much farther from any road than had been the case before. The ATC and the trail clubs' decision to remove or relocate shelters away from roads also cut down (but did not eliminate) the amount of partying at the shelters by non hikers. As the trail moved farther from roads and became less easily accessible to those who just wanted a place to drink, smoke and have some fun on a weekend night, the Appalachian Trail became more and more of a *hiker's* trail—a place where hikers went for however long they wanted to bathe in the beauty of the Appalachian forests, to test themselves, restore themselves, spend time with friends and family and renew their connections to nature.

The current version of the Appalachian Trail, the one we know, is all of those things, but with a further overlay. The AT has become a cultural touchstone—a *thing*—that people around the world have heard of, know something about and aspire to visit. With the advent of data phones, digital photography and most importantly social media, the Appalachian Trail has added another group of hikers—those who are there for the party, for the likes, the shares, the new friends made in a thru hiker (or attempted thru hiker) community that seems to grow a bit larger each year. Aggressive promotion of the thru hiking experience by the ATC, gear companies and communities along the trail have helped to grow this segment of the hiking public quite dramatically over the past fifteen years or so, to the point where trail club members are starting to talk about the Appalachian Trail being too crowded and too popular and saying things like, "Hikers are loving the Appalachian Trail to death." Some locations like McAfee Knob in Virginia or Max Patch Mountain in North Carolina are suffering from extreme overcrowding, but the places where overuse of the trail is evident are still thankfully few.

The COVID-19 pandemic certainly added to the number of hikers on the trail as people up and down the East Coast turned to the AT as a place they could get out of their houses, escape quarantine for a few hours or a few days and just forget about the pandemic for at least a bit. The pandemic crowds on the trail have ebbed, but the number of hikers overall seems to remain substantially larger than it was before the virus showed up in North America. All that growth in the number of hikers would have made the trail's founders and early builders quite happy. They were very concerned that they would put in all that work to build a trail from Georgia to Maine and that almost no one would hike on it. If they were around today, they might worry about the impact on the mountain ecosystems, or they might not love seeing quite so many people at and around trail shelters on popular weekends. But I'm quite certain they would have been happy to see their trail so heavily used.

I like to hike solo, a fact that makes my wife a bit nervous for the simple reason that I trip a lot when I walk. If I lifted my feet more, I wouldn't trip so much, but it's just how I hike. And I fall sometimes, so she worries. Not a lot. But some. I constantly reassure her that most sections of the Appalachian

Trail these days see lots of hikers between March and November, and so if I were to trip, fall and break something, *someone* would certainly come by within twenty-four hours and more likely within an hour or two. Given the growing ubiquity of cell service along the trail, my odds of being able to get a text out for help are pretty good as well. I say all this just to point out that not everything about the increasing number of hikers on the trail is a bad thing. Knowing that someone would eventually find me and rescue me gives me some solace and helps her worry a little less.

For most Appalachian Trail hikers, their revelatory moments, their emotional connections to wild places, last only for a few minutes or a few hours. For others, who return to the trail again and again for respite, for quiet and for peace, those experiences begin to aggregate, to take root within them, to create new spaces for renewal, for joy, for wonder. Benton MacKaye wanted the Appalachian Trail to be a place where people could "solve the problems of living." Despite the crowds, despite the challenges it faces, the AT remains a place where people can indeed find solutions to whatever ails them. And it's a place where hikers can still write, "I saw a bobcat! I saw a bobcat!"

Smell the earth.
No really.
Close your eyes and smell the earth,
Those first few raindrops
Which awaken the forest's aroma
The moisture in the air
And the damp ground
Combine to create a wonderful smell.
The smell of earth.

—anonymous hiker at the Blood Mountain Shelter in Georgia, 1991

FURTHER READING

Adcock, Trey. "Native Lands." *Journeys: The Magazine of the Appalachian Trail Conservancy* (Winter 2021).

Anderson, Larry. *Benton MacKaye: Conservationist, Planner, and Creator of the Appalachian Trail.* Johns Hopkins University Press, 2002.

Berg, Adam. "'To Conquer Myself': The New Strenuosity and the Emergence of 'Thru-Hiking' on the Appalachian Trail in the 1970s." *Journal of Sport History* 42, no. 1 (2015): 1–19.

Bryson, Bill. *A Walk in the Woods: Rediscovering America on the Appalachian Trail.* Anchor Books, 2006.

D'Anieri, Philip. *The Appalachian Trail: A Biography*. Mariner Books, 2021.

Decker, Sarah Jones. *The Appalachian Trail: Backcountry Shelters, Lean-Tos, and Huts*. Rizzoli, 2020.

Espy, Gene. *The Trail of My Life*. Indigo Publishing Group, 2008.

The Green Tunnel. Podcast, R2 Studios. https://www.r2studios.org/show/the-green-tunnel.

Hare, James R. *Hiking the Appalachian Trail.* 2 vols. Rodale Press, 1975.

Johnson, Thomas R. *From Dream to Reality: History of the Appalachian Trail.* Appalachian Trail Conservancy, 2021.

Kelly, Mills. "The A.T. and Race." *Journeys: The Magazine of the Appalachian Trail Conservancy* (Winter 2021).

———. "The Class of '51." *Appalachia* (Summer/Fall 2020): 24–33.

———. *Virginia's Lost Appalachian Trail.* The History Press, 2023.

King, Brian B. *The Appalachian Trail: Celebrating America's Hiking Trail.* Foreword by Bill Bryson. Rizzoli, 2012.

Luxenberg, Larry. *Walking the Appalachian Trail.* Stackpole Books, 1994.

Miller, Jason. "BackPacked Architecture: The Appalachian Trail and Its 'Primitive Huts.'" *Journal of Appalachian Studies* 21, no. 2 (2015): 247–62.

Mittlefehldt, Sarah. *Tangled Roots: The Appalachian Trail and American Environmental Politics.* University of Washington Press, 2013.

Montgomery, Ben. *Grandma Gatewood's Walk: The Inspiring Story of the Woman Who Saved the Appalachian Trail.* Chicago Review Press Inc., 2014.

Moor, Robert. *On Trails.* Simon & Schuster, 2016.

Ryan, Jeffrey H. *Blazing Ahead: Benton MacKaye, Myron Avery, and the Rivalry that Built the Appalachian Trail.* Appalachian Mountain Club Books, 2017.

INDEX

G

H

K

L

M

N

O

P

S

T

W

ABOUT THE AUTHOR

Mills Kelly is an emeritus professor of history at George Mason University in Fairfax, Virginia, and a historian of the Appalachian Trail. He began hiking on the trail as a young Boy Scout in 1971, and the trail has been part of his life ever since. Today, he is the maintainer of the Manassas Gap shelter along the trail in Northern Virginia, a board member of the Appalachian Trail Museum and the volunteer archivist of the Potomac Appalachian Trail Club. He is also the host of *The Green Tunnel* podcast, on the history of the Appalachian Trail. He is the author of several books, including *Virginia's Lost Appalachian Trail*, which tells the story of the original route of the AT in Southwest Virginia. He lives in Edenton, North Carolina, and also part time in Linden, Virginia, less than a mile from the trail.

Visit us at
www.historypress.com